General editor
Peter
Herriot

New
Essential
Psychology

Selves in
Relation

FORTHCOMING TITLES IN THIS SERIES

Information and Human Performance
Paul J. Barber and David Legge

Applying Psychology in Organizations
Frank Blackler and Sylvia Shimmin

Physiological Psychology
Theory and applications
John Blundell

Personality Theories and their Clinical Applications
Peter Fonagy

Social Interaction and its Management
Judy Gahagan

Cognitive Psychology
Judith Greene

Instinct, Environment and Behaviour
S.E.G. Lea

Experimental Design and Statistics
Second edition
Steve Miller

Multivariate Design and Statistics
Steve Miller

Individual Differences
Theories and applications
V.J. Shackleton and C.A. Fletcher

Lifespan Development
Concepts, theories and interventions
Léonie Sugarman

Cognitive Social Psychology and Social Policy
Kerry Thomas

Cognitive Development and Education
Johanna Turner

Learning Theory and Behaviour Modification
Stephen Walker

Keith Oatley

Selves in Relation

An introduction
to psychotherapy
and groups

Methuen   London and New York

First published in 1984 by
Methuen & Co. Ltd
11 New Fetter Lane, London EC4P 4EE

Published in the USA by
Methuen & Co.
in association with Methuen, Inc.
733 Third Avenue, New York, NY 10017

Typeset by Rowland Phototypesetting Ltd
Bury St Edmunds, Suffolk
Printed in Great Britain by
Richard Clay (The Chaucer Press) Ltd
Bungay, Suffolk

British Library
Cataloguing in Publication Data

Oatley, Keith
Selves in relation. –
(New essential psychology)
1. Group psychotherapy
I. Title   II. Series
616.89'152   RC488
ISBN 0-416-33630-2

Library of Congress
Cataloging in Publication Data

Oatley, Keith
Selves in relation.
(New essential psychology)
Bibliography: p.
Includes index.
1. Psychotherapist and patient.
2. Group psychotherapy.
I. Title.   II. Series
RC480.8.027   1984   616.89'152
83-19525
ISBN 0-416-33630-2 (pbk.)

Contents

Preface   vii

1   Prelude   1
2   Community   10
3   Individuality   30
4   The practice of psychotherapy   44
5   Outcome of therapy   73
6   The life of groups   88
7   The effects of groups   106
8   Personal learning in groups   120
9   Emotions and cultural experience   135

Suggestions for further reading   156
References and name index   158
Subject index   165

Preface

This book is about the relational issues of therapy. It is not about the different schools of therapy. It takes up the theme that is present in almost all of them: what goes on in the relationship between client and therapist, or between the members of a group?

The informing idea of the book is that therapy takes place in the interplay between client and therapist, in what Winnicott (1971) called a 'space', in between the self and another. It is a space in which things both are and are not what they seem, in which one is and is not oneself, and the other both is and is not who we imagine.

In the book I include four fragments of 'cases', by way of illustration. One is a disguised version of the story of someone I have seen in therapy. Two are fictional, and one, in the last chapter, is undisguised and not fictional. These fragments provide different perspectives on a common theme of disappointment.

I feel uneasy about case material in books. On the one hand it is necessary to particularize, and to clarify with paradigmatic examples. But on the other, in a typical case it is only the client who is presented, and who furthermore is portrayed as struggling and confused. The fact of a relation with a therapist seems to carry the complementary implication of a therapist who is secure and knowledgeable. This is not an accurate picture, much though some professionals would like it to be so. The therapist also struggles, and suffers from confusions. Moreover, in the meeting something important can take place not just for the client, but for both, or in a group for all. I do not know how to resolve this serious defect in presenting case fragments in which the client is the main focus, and for this I apologize.

My thanks most especially to Jenny Jenkins who discussed and commented on the book, page by page and chapter by chapter. Her suggestions have much improved it. Peter Smith and Peter Herriot read drafts of the whole book, and Judy Hildebrand read the chapters on groups, for which I thank them, and I am grateful for their valuable suggestions and comments. I am grateful to those who have taught me about therapy in various ways and at various times: Ben Churchill, Max Clowes, John Heaton, Ronnie Laing, Nancy MacKenzie, Chris Oakley, Haya Oakley, Tony Ryle, Peter Smith, Mary Welch, Paul Zeal and to the people whom I have met taking part in groups and therapy over the past ten years or so. I also thank the members of the Clinical and Psychotherapy Seminar at Sussex with whom matters such as these have been discussed over the last three years, and the Sussex students who read drafts of chapters of the book and commented on them: Philip Carroll, Pat Cook, Julie Daniel, Chris Fiford, Margaret Fyffe, Lynette Humphrey, Richard Mullen, David Panter, Sue Raymond, Brad Roter, Iain Travers and Jenny Trust.

KEITH OATLEY

1

Prelude

Psychotherapy has taken place in different cultures throughout history. It is an activity in which people who have become disablingly distressed, discouraged or frightened, or who feel themselves no longer to be themselves, renew their own life and rejoin the life of their community.

Many of the forms which we might now call 'therapy' have been religious. They have included practices that a person cultivates alone, like meditation; departures from the ordinary routines of life, like going on a pilgrimage; meetings with another person such as a shaman, confessor or guru; gatherings and celebrations of a community, like festivals or the theatre.

This book is mainly about the relational aspects of therapy. In states of disabling distress the person's relationship with him or herself is disrupted and so is the relationship with others. It is therefore the starting-point of this book that it is in the relation with others that healing is to be sought. 'To heal' comes from the old English word 'hale' meaning 'whole'. And this quest for wholeness is close to many people's deepest wish in entering therapy. They embark on therapy because they are feeling scattered, not themselves, cut off from others.

Therapy is fundamentally an ethical activity: a search for right relationship, or as Buddhist practice has it, right action. This does not just mean authenticity, though it involves that. On its own that could degenerate into self-absorption. Neither is it simply living inconspicuously within the rules and customs of the community. On its own that might just become compliance and emptiness. Rather, right action involves personal authenticity within the rules and customs of a community, a right relation with oneself and with others. It involves truth rather than self-deception, and it involves engagement in one's interactions, rather than simply going through the motions.

There are two broad categories: individual therapy, where just one person meets with a therapist, and group therapy, where several people meet.

The distinction between individual and group therapy does not correspond to the question of the relation with oneself and with others. Philosophers have taught us that relations with oneself and with others are not easily dissociated. A person feels disturbed and distressed, when aspects of his or her actions, thoughts and feelings seem alien, and just happen without being willed. At the same time the person typically is also disturbing to others.

Therapy either individually or in groups involves taking part with the other in a relationship which might be healing. It can allow the self and relationships to become more whole, less a set of fragments, each engaged in keeping some particular aspect of the world at bay. By taking part in a therapeutic relationship the person can become less prone to the suffering and deceits which such fragmentation involves.

Individuality and community

There is a fundamental question with which therapy is concerned. It is how far we are primarily individuals, who happen to meet others in the course of our lives and enter into various kinds of social arrangements with them; or how far social being is primary and we take our life from the community of family, friends and culture around us. Are we individuals primarily, and social only secondarily? Or is our individual experience and consciousness secondary to the communities in which we take part? These questions pervade the therapeutic enterprise – for if we are primarily individuals, then what is important might be to find ways of changing the individual. Whereas if we discover ourselves primarily in relationships then it is within the relationships, not the individual, that transformation is to be sought.

This distinction is so fundamental, that I have built the structure of the book around it, taking alternate perspectives from the individual and the community. So, apart from this chapter and the final one, which are opening and closing brackets, and are written from my perspective as writer, the other chapters juxtapose individual and community views. Chapters 2–5 are mainly about one-to-one therapy, whereas chapters 6–8 are about groups. Chapter 2 is in the 'communal' voice, which I shall take to be female, and the main personal pronouns will be 'she' and 'her'. Chapter 3 is in an 'individual' voice, and singular personal pronouns will be male. This arrangement of alternating chapters continues up to chapter 8.

There is a tension between the individual and the communal, between the one and the many, between issues of personal authenticity and the membership of society which is central to the concerns of therapy. Often, for instance, the desire of an individual conflicts with the rules of the community that person lives in. The person may alternate between his or her own impulses and conformity to the requirements of society, and experience the conflicts as distressing.

In more severe disrelations with self and others that occur in emotional crises, these themes of individuality and communality often come uppermost – for instance a man's devotion to his work, his ambition, may lead to his wife leaving him, and his family breaking up. Alternatively a woman's devotion to her family while neglecting her own individuality might lead to a sense of futility, or of barely suppressed resentment which finally leads to a similar breakup.

Bakan (1966) in his book *The Duality of Human Existence* writes of this tension between the individual and the communal, arguing that in western society we have swayed too far in the direction of individuality, the mark of which he calls unrestrained agency, the use of power unremitted by any concern for the other, which is familiar to us in wars and a variety of coercive relations.

3

Two perspectives

Lest the notion of individual and communal perspectives seems obscure, consider a scene: a group of people eating a meal, that most familiar of human activities. How could it be described in some such way as to bring the unity, the community of this event, into the foreground?

It might be seen as a family: a name that designates a history of life together and a shared culture created together from which each person takes his or her own sense of being.

It could be seen as ritual, a ceremonial enactment of human society in the sharing of food.

It could be seen as a kind of game, defined and given meaning by the rules of the microculture of that group: the rules in which it is known perhaps that to eat everything given is to compliment the cook, or in which it is known that men sit and talk while women clear away dishes – rules by which meaning is given to action, in their observance as well as in their breaking.

It could be seen almost as a kind of dance or a piece of music, in which the structure of what occurs has harmonies and dissonances, a kind of attunement of the parts with each other.

It could be seen as system, in which the interaction of parts is generative of the behaviour of the whole, rather than functions of the whole being embodied separately in individual parts.

It could be described as a story, a tale of how these people came together to be like this.

All those images are of wholes, of groups: where what is named first is the whole structure – only secondarily its parts whose being is in the life of the whole. But this language is slightly unfamiliar in our culture when it comes to talking of ourselves. We prefer to see ourselves as individuals who perhaps meet, who do things; occasionally do things to each other: love, hate, bargain, listen to, abandon, as if in our selfhood we were separate, enclosed in bubbles. We might bump up against others in our trajectories through life, but remain forever isolated. What is between us is spoken of as if we are previously defined objects which stand or move into or out of relation to each other.

So the same meal could be observed in an individual perspective, when this person or that person is seen to display his or her personality, or perhaps to interact with others.

4

Someone sits next to an old friend, and they exchange gossip.

Another person might be seen to be uncomfortable, ill at ease, and not joining in the conversation.

Yet another person is happy, expansive and talkative.

Perhaps a mother tries to persuade her daughter to eat the food she has been given.

Maybe one person flirts with another. Might that perhaps cause the uncomfortableness of one of the other participants?

One might wonder whether there is anything wrong with the daughter whose mother is trying to make her eat.

Each one of us might be one of these people, with our own preoccupations, motives, abilities, feelings, thoughts.

We experience ourselves and others quite differently according to how we talk, describe and perceive. It is not either as individuals or as society that we discover ourselves, it is between society and the individual that human life arises. Not that we are cogs in a machine called society. Not that we are individuals who have these or those purposes, and then have to find ways of co-ordinating our actions with others. Rather, that human being emerges from the interplay of community and individual experience.

And psychotherapy? Therapy is the struggle of two or more people 'to recover the wholeness of being human through the relationship between them' (Laing, 1967, p. 45). Though even here, as one might notice, the assumption is that we are individuals who might meet in a relationship. The view from the other position is that we recover our humanity by taking part in a community that already exists, rather than absenting ourselves into isolation.

Indirect communication

Matters having to do with human relating can only be referred to, not spoken of directly. One could no more tell someone what being in love is like than explain colours to a blind person. So to write of love or hate, or of disappointment or renewal, I must rely on resonating with the reader's experiences of these things, hoping to evoke them in various interrelations with each other, so that they might form into new structures of meaning.

To speak or write about therapy is a paradoxical activity. It can't be done, at least not directly. Plato (for example in his VIIth letter) was acutely aware of this, arguing that it was not really possible to tell people anything they did not already know, or which at least was not on the threshold of being realized. The chief protagonist in his writings, Socrates, describes himself not as a teacher, or an adviser, but as a midwife, being on hand to ease the birth of knowledge, insight, understanding, truth.

Plato has given us a portrait of one of the first psychotherapists. Socrates would go around the market-place, starting conversations with people in a way which was experienced by them as both strange and as moving. As Alcibiades says in Plato's *Symposium*, Socrates's words 'stir up the depths' (p. 100). And this is the mark of therapy: it is usually conducted entirely verbally, but it does not give information, it is not rhetoric or persuasion, but it touches us and moves us. It takes place within a relationship which not only is meaningful of itself but also resonates with our other important relationships, 'stirring us to the depths'.

Right action – what the Greeks called 'the good' – cannot be transmitted by writing it down, or commanding people to do this or that. Plato supposed that it emerged, almost like a forgotten memory, between people in certain kinds of relationship such as between lovers, or in conversations such as the ones Socrates struck up. Nevertheless Plato wrote voluminously. He did not write his 'philosophy'; he knew that philosophy, the love of wisdom, was not like that. To learn off by heart the 'philosophy' of a teacher might make one into a superior kind of parrot, but not a philosopher.

So Plato's writings about Socrates, and wisdom, and love and society, are not in the form of a textbook. They are dialogues, offering an image, of what it might have been like to take part oneself in a discussion with Socrates.

Socrates, moreover, is not necessarily right. What is important is that the reader, or the person taking part in the dialogue, or the client in therapy, can enter a state of his or her *own* reflections. Thereby he or she might come to realizations which are his or her own, that is which are authentic, not just taken up under the pressure of 'ought', or for exams, or to please the other, or to show off.

This psychotherapy book is not a dialogue. However the alternating chapters from the individual and communal perspectives are juxtaposed, rather bluntly, in order to allow reflection.

The book has passages which give information, for example on various theories, and particularly on the empirical findings of the effects and effectiveness of therapy, that is chapters 5 and 7. It is much more textbookish than anything Plato would have approved of.

If I am at all successful the reader will construct or discover his or her own theory of therapy, drawn mainly from experience of living and relating, and perhaps helped into the world by the juxtapositions and ideas which reading can summon up. *Theoria* for the Pythagorean Greeks meant an engaged contemplation, such as one might find oneself engrossed in as participant at a festival. It helps to have had some of one's own therapy, or to have been to a group, in order to form one's own theory. If not, however, the matters with which therapy deals are sufficiently part of the texture of ordinary life to have touched most people in western culture.

Therapy is a process of relating with another or others in which, rather than re-enacting the usual things, and experiencing others as we usually do, something different can emerge. Therapy is a relationship which might make a difference, which might allow one to know oneself and the other.

To know oneself

'Know thyself' was written up in the temple of Apollo in Delphi some 2500 years ago. In Plato's *Phaedrus*, Socrates poking fun at some of the rarefied intellectual antics of the Sophists, perhaps the equivalent of today's university types, says he himself hasn't time for such pursuits. 'I have not yet succeeded' he says, 'in obeying the Delphic injunction to "know myself"' (p. 25).

To know oneself is to be able to act responsibly, in relation both to oneself and others. Mental distress, sometimes called mental illness, is at least partly due to people not knowing themselves, being in disrelation with themselves and with others. People feel attacked by feelings of grief or irritation or panic which seem to have nothing to do with them. They say they would like to be able to do this or that but cannot.

The radical idea of psychotherapy is that although people experience all these things as coming from outside them, or at least as being beyond their will or control, and one has no reason to

doubt them – it is they who do these things to themselves. Because they have disowned various aspects of themselves, what they do and feel has become alien and obscure. Knowing oneself involves knowing what one is doing to oneself, and to others.

No one could possibly hope to abolish suffering and misery in the world, but as Freud (1895) said, what could be hoped for is that therapy might help turn 'hysterical misery into common unhappiness' (p. 393). And this takes place, in a relation with another.

However therapy is, in a way, not special. The most important therapy is life, and the most important therapists one's friends. But a therapeutic crisis in life, a turning-point, is also called a nervous breakdown. When such breakdowns are destructive rather than constructive, or when the rigidity of patterns or the restrictions of life are increasing, therapists can be of help.

A client for therapy

In order to talk about therapy I have imagined a client, Ms Cindy S, part of whose story I will tell at various junctures in the book.

Cindy is 25. She is not in paid employment but she would like to get a job or train for a career. She lives with her husband Bob, who is an insurance salesman, and spends nearly all her time at home, though she does not like being alone, particularly when it is dark. She also hates going out alone, and will go out only when accompanied by her husband or her mother. She hasn't been out alone for six years, since she suffered a terrifying experience when she was shopping. Her heart started pounding, and she felt a sense of dread much worse than anything she thought could be experienced. Though she felt she was going to die she did not lose consciousness, but hurried home, phoned her husband, who came home from work and then took her to the doctor. She has been having treatment for her heart intermittently ever since, and is diagnosed as having a hyperkinetic heart syndrome. There had been some question of her having trouble with her heart during her childhood. She has had other attacks since the first one, and came to fear even stepping outside the front door on her own. Her husband takes her out, though they do not go out often. She can't eat out or even have a cup of tea in a café, as she feels it will make her sick. But they do household shopping together on Saturdays, and sometimes go for drives together. She can usually persuade her mother to go shopping for clothes during the week, which she enjoys. For the most part she stays at home, does housework, listens to records. She occasionally feels suicidal, and that she will never be able to do anything, because of her heart. Though she would like to get a job she does not think she would be strong enough physically to do it.

Here is a woman whose life is a problem: she suffers terror and despair which overwhelm her, and which she has no control of, she has plans and aspirations but cannot carry them out. The bright point apparently is that though she has no other friends, she has a husband who is devoted to her and looks after her.

It is just such a person who might seek therapy. Indeed Cindy did. She asked her doctor, who referred her to a clinical psychologist. She was keen to undertake therapy because she thought it might make it possible to get a job, or train for a career.

I will return from time to time to Cindy's story as an illustration. But first to some ideas of the structures of community, which seem less visible than the structures of individuality.

2

Community

Though it is clear that in the western world we like to think of ourselves as individuals, individual authors of actions, and individual experiencers, it is less clear that this is good for us. As Bateson (1971) points out, in cutting down a tree the 'average Occidental . . . says "I cut down the tree" and he even believes that there is a delimited agent, the "self", which performed a delimited "purposive" action upon a delimited object' (p. 288). There is, however, the possibility of seeing this action not as one agent doing something to an object, but as a system of interaction. Bateson's alternative is:

> Each stroke of the axe is modified or corrected, according to the shape of the cut . . . this self corrective (i.e. mental) process is brought about by a total system, tree-eyes-brain-muscles-axe-stroke-tree; and it is this total system that has the characteristics of immanent mind. (p. 288)

'Immanent' is a term scarcely used outside philosophy. It means 'indwelling' or 'inherent'. Bateson asserts that mind is inherent not in the person, but in the activity of the system of differences that tree and person are making to each other in their interaction. This is a different way of knowing from the normal western one. It is so odd as to seem absurd – the idea of mind as inherent in our interacting in the world; not something in the head of an individual in which thoughts, feelings and motives might be found. Mind is not in any of the parts of the system, or even in the system itself. It emerges in the interaction.

We do not have much of a language to speak articulately in these terms. For this reason Koestler (1979) coined the term 'holon' – from the Greek 'holos' meaning 'whole', but with 'on' at the end implying a part. So holon is a part of the whole. Each whole is made up of the interacting parts. According to Minuchin and Fishman (1981):

> Every holon – the individual, the nuclear family, the extended family, and the community – is both a whole and a part, not more one than the other. . . . Each whole contains the part, and each part contains the 'program' that the whole imposes. Part and whole contain each other in a continuing, current, and ongoing process of communication and interrelationship. (p. 13)

The idea that self is wider than our individual body has many implications. The most important, in the context of therapy, is that the wider scope of selfhood is the activity of our relating with others. But though we discover ourselves in participation, we are often prevented from participating by pressing preoccupations, remnants of earlier 'programs', which can become so distressing that they become psychiatric symptoms. Such symptoms both spoil our participation, and themselves demand that the rules of interaction be changed.

The disowned as part of the mental

First, then, to seeing the apparently external as participating in the mental: W.H. Auden remarked that one shouldn't ask people whether they have read any good books lately; it's better to ask if they have been read by any good books. If the book is at all good we are taken up into its world. Our experience is shaped by it much more than anything we do to it in reading it. It seems that in the process of developing the image of ourselves as individuals we see ourselves as the sole authors of actions, the sole knowers.

Bateson spent much time arguing that the idea of individuals controlling their environments is not just mistaken, but dangerous – not just in relation to people, though here it is perhaps at its most dangerous, but in relation to the natural world as well. As what we take to be self shrinks to include only what is inside the skin, that which is outside the skin is non-self, and hence is alien and potentially hostile.

We persist in thinking that a 'self' is a kind of conscious thing which Watts (1966) called the 'skin encapsulated ego'. We create ourselves as lonely individuals, struggling to assert control over that which we see as outside us, and which therefore has to be subdued or repelled.

Bateson points out that the future of a species in this kind of relationship with its environment, and in these kinds of relationships among its members, does not look hopeful.

So where is the error in what we think we know to be our selves? It is partly, says Bateson (1970), in not seeing that it is differences that make a difference. Differences not things. Thingification, more formally called 'reification', makes both the self and the other into things. To concentrate on differences might remind us of relationship, and of the flow of interaction.

In the interaction of tree-felling, it is the difference between the position of the axe and the wedge-shaped cut which guides the axe, which makes a difference to the tree, which is seen as a difference which guides the difference in the swing of the axe, and so on. The circuit is of differences, and it goes beyond the skin. A difference, moreover, says Bateson, is abstract. There are differences visible between the black of the ink on this page and the white of the paper. The differences make the letters readable. The difference is not in the ink (obviously), nor in the paper (obviously). Differences are not in things at all and yet it is they that make a difference to us. To trace the path of differences is moreover to leave the skin and include the environment within the circuit.

Imagine for instance, in another of Bateson's images, a blind man with a stick walking and tapping along the pavement. Does the man end at the tip of the stick? At the handle? No, the activity of walking has to be seen as person and environment, not just for blind people but for everybody. And to cut the circuit so that only part of it is seen as significant is an error. We need at least to see ourselves as parts of our various worlds, physical and social.

The alternative is an arrogant notion of power and control over that which is outside the skin – since that becomes defined as 'not self', therefore needing to be kept in order by the only agent that we take to be capable of acting in the interest of the self, namely the self.

Bateson tells the story of J.S. Bach who when asked how he played so divinely said, 'I play the notes in order as they are written. It is God who makes the music' (1970, pp. 437–8). We might see this nowadays as quaint, if in our culture the only agent is self inside a skin. But to do so would be *hubris*, that sin known to the Greeks of trespassing on the preserves of gods: the sin of arrogating all mind to self, the sin which invites *nemesis*.

If our image or theory of our self is of a separation into delimited causes and things, our being will be correspondingly in error.

Ourselves as holons in interaction

Although our relation with the natural world is fundamental, it is our social relations which for the human species become at least equally important, and much more problematic. So how might we take the step of acquiring a communal perspective, of seeing ourselves as parts of social interactions, as partaking in them. The language of our ordinary world is not totally devoid of the holistic idea. We know it takes two for company, three for jealousy. In some ways we know that a drama or story emerges in interaction, and that selves of various kinds are discovered in the interaction, rather than being preformed and fixed before coming to it.

We even have in our society specific forms of rule-governed interaction, which have the sole purpose of bestowing a certain kind of experience on their participants. They are called games and playing. We take part in such activities entirely for the sake of taking part in them. Therein lies the 'Fun in Games', as Erving Goffman (1961) has entitled a famous essay. As he argues in that essay, if we could see how games are fun, then maybe we could understand how experience is engendered in participation in serious as well as less serious activities.

In a game, be it hide-and-seek, tennis, a game at a children's party or an encounter group, a flirtation or a conversation, there are two broad classes of consideration.

One has to do with the rules of the game: rules, or customs by which the game is defined and instantiated. The second has to do with the participants and their engagement in the game.

The rules of a game provide the furniture of a specific world of that game: the structures of possible events in which meaning will be generated. In chess a player does not shift a wooden object 3 centimetres in a north-easterly direction, though she might advance her king's pawn one square. It is only within the rules of chess that such actions have meaning, and it is the rules that provide the basis for generating meanings within the game.

But as Goffman points out, the rules alone do not have this power. It requires the participation of players in the roles afforded by the game, players who intend to attack on the queen's side in chess; or whose sense of anticipatory excitement mounts in hide-and-seek as the footsteps of the seeker are heard approaching. So the rules of the game allow for participation in the role of player with both knowledge and intentions, whose experience will emerge in the game.

Goffman talks of the rules and the participatory roles as follows:

> A matrix of possible events and a cast of roles through whose enactment the events occur constitute together a field for fateful dramatic action, a plane of being, an engine of meaning, a world in itself, different from all other worlds except the ones generated when the same game is played at other times. (p. 27)

Games and serious activities all have this quality, suggests Goffman. We constitute our worlds through sets of rules and take part in the roles afforded by them. The main difference between the activities that we call games and those we take to be serious are that in games we have a right to expect to enjoy them. We take delight in the experience generated in whatever micro-world we have chosen to enter. We might enjoy either the exploitation of another player or fending off bankruptcy in Monopoly. In what we take to be serious activities similar events might seem much less enjoyable, though they take us up into the experience that they afford in a similar kind of way.

It is not the individual who comes already equipped with all the properties of experiencing, and just happens to interact with others. As with the chopping of the tree, it is from interaction that characteristics emerge. Human characteristics are language, drama, stories, personality, mind, experience. . . .

The vitality of participation

We often come to therapy because we do not feel fully alive. The idea of holons, of being parts of interacting wholes, offers an explanation: 'It's not surprising if we turn ourselves and others into things.' When self is a kind of thing, it will feel dead. Vitality is participation, and Goffman (1961) offers a theory of how human meaning and vitality emerge by participation in rule-governed activities like games and social life. His major theme is that to have fun in games, one must be involved, not just enacting the rules of the game as an anonymous agent. One must have one's heart in it.

Engrossment and engagement

Goffman opens his essay with a rather tasteless speech of Fainall from William Congreve's play *The Way of the World* (1700): a riposte to his partner, Mirabel, who had offered to go on playing cards to entertain:

> No, I'll give you your revenge another time, when you are not so indifferent. . . . I'd no more play with a man that slighted his ill-fortune, than I'd make love to a woman who undervalued the loss of her reputation. (Act I, scene i)

Children also know how to counter a particularly disadvantageous proposal with, 'All right then I won't play', knowing how this deflates everything.

But to be unengrossed in certain kinds of activity is dreadful for oneself too. Not to take part is to feel empty and futile, as well as being disturbing for the other who may become angry and rejecting, like Fainall.

Fainall became sarcastic because playing cards was a way of engaging his friend Mirabel in engrossed participation. He makes the nasty remark about a woman's 'loss of reputation', because he senses Mirabel's less than whole-hearted engagement, and love-making is perhaps the most compelling example of the interaction in which, in our society, engrossment is at its most necessary. As

Goffman goes on to point out, in love-making the degree of engrossment is seen by both partners as a test of the relationship. Local happenings are testing in their power to distract either of the partners. Formulated as a game it is clear that time-out cannot be declared, substitutes cannot ordinarily be brought on, and certain kinds of non-attention can be lethal.

In general the success of an interaction depends on the degree of involvement that the participants generate. Each participant brings in certain considerations and preoccupations, personal accoutrements having to do with recent or more distant history. But if some of these are not suppressed then the encounter is sabotaged. So for instance, as Goffman points out, two ex-husbands of the same woman must suppress considerations that they cannot entirely banish or they spoil all possibility of inter-action with one another.

The semi-permeable membrane

In Goffman's perspective, each participation, each gathering is game-like in that it has certain rules which will be capable of sustaining the meanings of what may happen. To pass into such a gathering is to pass through a kind of semi-permeable membrane. Within it only such considerations as are relevant to the encounter can be allowed expression. To be engaged in the gathering within the membrane is to be participating. One's life and experience emerge in what goes on. But inevitably participants import more than their willingness to engage in the gathering. Like the two ex-husbands of the same woman, they might have preoccupations, generated either spontaneously or triggered off by the meeting itself.

Goffman points out that when some extraneous issue has passed with us through the semi-permeable membrane, it is precisely that kind of material which disturbs the flow of inter-action. It may be felt by the importer of the material as a painful embarrassment, and by others as a disruption of their engagement in the interaction. Such intrusions seem involuntary, and they constitute symptoms for which people seek therapy.

In one of Goffman's examples we see an intrusion of this kind in a mental hospital when 'a patient at meal time asks for the salt in a voice that covers the whole table with misery and gloom' (p. 24).

The patient is unable to sustain the encounter with the ordinary rules of having a meal. The failure of this person to do so is not just felt as a trivial issue, like Mirabel not feeling like playing cards. It has the most serious implications for all concerned. The patient finds it impossible to take part in almost any engagement with others because of pressing preoccupation. Meetings with such a person are regularly broken up by such a non-participation. People find they can only engage in meetings centred round such a person's misery. A psychiatrist who sees this type of infraction of social rules sees it as a symptom to be relieved, brought under control.

It is, as Goffman says, the joint definition of a situation in terms of unspoken rules that people experience as reality. 'That other persons are involved ensures that engrossment must be steadily sustained in spite of the flickering of one's actual interest.' It is the engrossed participation both of oneself and the other in what we are doing that either brings the world constructed from the rules of the encounter alive, or, by failure to sustain the engrossment, can 'shrivel up the reality in which one is lodged' (p. 41).

Out of mind or out of play?

Freud's account of psychiatric symptoms was that they emerged meaningfully but disguised, from the unconscious: symptoms consist of 'material which, although pushed away by consciousness, has nevertheless not been robbed of all capacity for expressing itself' (1901, p. 344). Freud showed how serious neurotic symptoms were built on the same structure as the more trivial errors and slips of everyday life, which can then intrude to disturb our sense that we are coping and in control of things. Goffman's (1961) book is partly a reworking of Freud's individualistic account of *The Psychopathology of Everyday Life* (1901), but in a communal perspective, in terms of people as holons in interaction.

Freud (1916–17) saw the mind as an individual space, with two compartments, like rooms. In one, a small drawing-room, resides consciousness, in the other larger entrance hall, thoughts, desires and impulses jostle.

But on the threshold between these two rooms a watchman performs his function: he examines the different mental impulses, acts as a censor, and will not admit them into the drawing room if they displease him. (p. 336)

If we take up Goffman's communal perspective, the properties of what goes right and what goes wrong in people's lives cease to be a matter of the mechanisms of the individual mind. They are matters of social engagement. The question becomes whether it is more or less easy to engage oneself in what one is doing. People may or may not find it possible to follow the rules of a social encounter. Under the stress of difficulties or preoccupations they may wish to withdraw from interaction, or else to control the situation by imposing new definitions of the rules of interaction on others.

Lapses which Goffman calls 'incidents' occur where the smooth flow of interaction is suddenly interrupted. For instance, a 'leaky word' which has a double meaning may embarrass both a black and a white person talking together when one of them utters the cliché 'things look very black'. The leaky word has allowed the importation across the semi-permeable barrier, of the question of skin colour, defined as irrelevant to the encounter, because in ordinary language 'black' is a common metaphor for the bad.

More violent is when, as Goffman says, someone 'floods out' – unable to contain the pressures of participating in the gathering and a more personal significance overwhelms her. Whether like the depressed patient asking for the salt to be passed, or 'Whether the individual bursts out crying or laughing, whether he erupts into open anger, shame, impatience, boredom or anguish, he radically alters his general support of the interaction, he is momentarily "out of play"' (p. 55).

Ms Cindy S's agoraphobic symptoms started with 'flooding out', in panic attacks, in which she felt overwhelmed by the impossibility of sustaining the interactions she was taking part in: when shopping, or alone among strangers, who she felt, were both hostile and expected her to behave with poise. She found she could keep the possibility of flooding out at bay by either staying at home, or by having her mother or husband to accompany her, by maintaining as it were a safe community of two, to fend off the larger community of potentially hostile others.

For people who do not succeed in keeping the possibility of flooding out at bay by means of this kind, the tension of holding a difficult interaction together, perhaps over a period of years, can

18

constitute a chronic anxiety, responsible for encroachment of despair and disintegration.

Acquiring one's part in the play

Part of the question raised by therapy is how the influence of wholes of which we have been part extend their effects long beyond the time when such modes of interaction were generated, and sometimes long beyond the time when they could possibly be relevant. In Freud's terms the question is what is this repressed material which returns in disguise from the unconscious. In Goffman's terms what are the preoccupations and considerations which we import inappropriately through the semi-permeable membranes of our interactions?

So powerful is the effect of intrusive material, that often what we take to be a self seems not to emerge from our desires, temperament and role in the current interaction at all, but to be a product largely of earlier patterns of interaction in the families of our origin. As Minuchin and Fishman (1981) said in their discussion of holons: it's not just that wholes contain parts, but 'each part contains the "program" that the whole imposes'. What can go wrong is that this programme is not necessarily a programme of rules appropriate to our current interaction. Many of people's reasons for seeking therapy are that they feel keenly the inappropriateness of what they import with them from much earlier interactions.

Mead's ideas of 'I' and 'me'

An important geographer of some of the territory of social selfhood was G.H. Mead. Along with the object-relations school of psychoanalysts he suggested how the individual, in Minuchin and Fishman's phrase, takes on the 'program of the whole' of which she is part. To start with, what is taken on is a pattern of rules of family interaction.

Mead first distinguished between 'I', who acts and experiences, and 'me' the term we use to indicate being objects to ourselves.

The experiencing 'I' cannot be an object, not a thing of any kind. It cannot itself be experienced, since it is the act of experiencing. Yet we do refer to ourselves as a kind of thing; for instance to seeing ourselves as others see us, or to being hard on ourselves, or to looking after ourselves. In such usages of language as these, self is not subject but object, and as such Mead called it 'me'.

But if 'I' means acting and experiencing and is not able to be the object of experience as such, then 'me' which can be an object of experience must be something else. It was for this that Cooley (1902) proposed the idea of the looking-glass self.

Our self, in a way, is doubly constituted. There is the 'I' of interaction and experience, but we also take ourselves to be 'me', which is really an image of self as seen reflected in what we imagine to be the eyes of others.

Mead supposed that it is in language that this second self, the 'me' comes into being. The actions of others are not enough to form a distinct reflection for us. Their words are more powerful and more definitive. 'You *are* a good girl to go to bed when Mummy tells you', 'How pretty you are when you take the trouble to brush your hair', and so on.

Although one might feel that this first self, the 'I' of experiencing and participation with others would be important, or even pre-eminent in our sense of self, this is not what happens. It is the much less fluid, more thing-like 'me', a codified and reflected image, which, in our society, we come to feel as ourself. And though this 'me' is essential both for technical planning, and as an internalization of social rules and customs, it also tends to have the isolation, and the arrogant pretensions which Bateson points out.

Although Mead is right to call it 'me', because we identify it with our self, its perspective is not of the first person 'I' or the second person 'you', who might take part in engaged interaction together. It is grammatically a third-person self, like 'she' or 'he': an image of self seen from the perspective of a judgemental non-participant observer.

It is this 'me-self' who carries preoccupations in through the semi-permeable membrane of our encounters, making it less easy for us to participate in them.

Mead proposed developmental stages by which the internalization of the programmes for our social existence occurs. 'Me' becomes an important mental object, because as Mead says it is an internalization of what starts off as the attitudes of the most important others in our lives. 'Inner consciousness is socially organized by the importation of the social organization of the outer world' (1912, p. 141). If in the outer world we are treated as good if we go to bed when told to, the sense of being good when we act as the other demands is organized anew in the structure of our consciousness, and in what we take to be ourself. 'I'm good when I do what the other wants.' It's not a long step to the life project of finding out what the other wants in order to do it, and thereby being able to think myself a good person.

The first stage in internalization is dramatic, rather like an early Greek drama. The child thinks about his 'conduct as good or bad only as he reacts to his own acts in the remembered words of his parents'. 'Me' is a 'fusion of the remembered actor and this accompanying chorus' (p. 147).

The second stage is play too, but of a different kind. Here the child starts to take on 'the roles of those who belong to his society' and play-acts 'a parent, a teacher, a preacher, a grocery man, a pirate, or an Indian'. In such play Mead supposed that the child both imitates and 'calls out in himself the same response as he calls out in the other'. So the self is not just awareness of initiating an act, but according to Mead, inherently social. 'Me' is the symbolically internalized act-and-its-response-in-the-other. So in playing with a doll the child 'responds in tone of voice and in attitude as his parents respond to his own cries and chortles' (p. 285).

In the third stage play is still the medium, but now in more organized games in which there is 'a regulated procedure and rule . . . the child must not only take the role of the other . . . but he must assume the various roles of all the participants in the game, and govern his actions accordingly' (p. 285). So when waiting to catch a ball in a game it is as one to whom the ball will be thown or hit by another player. The child plays in turn in the various roles afforded by the game, and in so doing builds up a skilled and rehearsed sense of the organized reactions to each role which are generated in the game. These organized reactions of social others which Mead has called 'the generalized other' then come to accompany and control conduct. 'It is this generalized other in his experience which provides him with a self' (p. 285).

Despite Bateson's strictures, there is nothing wrong in any of this. For 'me' to have internalized the rules and customs of the community 'I' am in is essential, otherwise I could not take part. What seems more of a struggle for us all, is to come to realize that this precipitate of previous relating (as Freud, 1923, called it) is neither fixed for all time, nor the whole of my self inside a skin.

Object-relations theory

Themes similar to Mead's emerge in psychoanalysis, starting with Freud's (1923) postulation of the super-ego, precipitate of each nuclear family's own social drama of *Oedipus Rex*. A relationship at first social, between the little boy and his father, in which the father prohibits the longings of the son for his mother, becomes internalized as a voice which criticizes and forbids, on pain of having something important taken away. The effect of the voice is present continuously, though it sinks below the level of awareness. As Mead put it, the voice of the Greek chorus to the early child's performances 'fades out' of awareness. By adulthood the 'emphasis falls on the meaning of the inner speech, the imagery becomes the barely necessary social cues' (1913, p. 147). The slight cue, for instance, of another's approval or of not responding to something we say, can plunge us into childhood feelings of elation or failure, though by now their origin in images of early performances has faded.

Later psychoanalytic writers such as Fairbairn (1952), Guntrip (1969) and Winnicott (1979) extended this idea which has become known as object-relations theory. According to this theory the centre of psychological life is relatedness to others. Where an other has become significant, she acquires for psychoanalysts the dreadful term 'object' as in the phrase 'object of my affections'.

The main idea of object-relations theory is that unsatisfactory relationships, involving threat or disappointment by significant others, are those which are most difficult to remember, but which are most firmly entrenched as internalizations of early unsatisfactory relationships. Both parts of an unsatisfactory relationship are internalized: the significant other person becomes a frightening image of potential threat or disappointment, while the self's role is set up as strategy for dealing with this threat or disappointment. Such internalized modes of relating can become fixed, and overwhelmingly large aspects of 'me'. They become, as it were, implicit theories about how to relate, to which, for the person concerned, there seem to be no alternatives.

Object-relations theorists start from the idea that the self is at first whole. But inevitably disappointments occur. Inevitably, for instance, a mother does not live up to what was imagined or expected of her. The infant self is unable to cope with the possibility that the same mother who is gratifying is also disappointing. Such primordial experiences of hatred are literally intolerable. The infant self therefore splits into pieces. It splits off its image of the bad, frustrating mother, splits off too its strategies of dealing with this frustrating mother. Instead of having a unitary self, experiencing and taking part in the relationship with its mother, the child's self is fragmented, with pieces separate from one another, as when in a rage one can no longer remember that the person with whom one is so furious is or ever has been at all lovable.

The split-off images of the bad mother are precisely not able to be thought about. They are repressed. What is left is the withdrawn, the defiant, the sulking, the frustrated or bad senses of self who have played opposite frustrating images of the unsatisfactory other; these senses of self in some circumstances come to be 'me', even though by now the original self is splintered into these or other particles, giving their owner a sense of disconnection and of something wrong.

Fairbairn argued that there tend to be two main splits. One is the split in which the mother is expected to be satisfying but is not. Thus the bad image of her is seen as seductive but frustrating while the complementary self feels disappointed as it resorts to strategies such as withdrawal. In the other the mother is seen as punitive, and the self is felt partly as an unsatisfactory, bad or unwanted child, perhaps then becoming rebellious. These dramatic scripts between the supposedly seductive or threatening other and the corresponding expecting-to-be-disappointed or frightened child are then played out when triggered off, and then used to make sense of various actions of others in the adult world. An action of someone one meets who had never agreed to be gratifying but who fails to do what we expect, can be felt as disappointing in the way prescribed by this early script.

In many cases people can, without really knowing why, spend large parts of their lives engaging others in the scripts provided by these early painful interactions, in order perhaps to try to bring them under control.

Distress and symptoms emerge then, as we struggle to work out

23

with current others, some of the unsatisfactory scripts of the past. To do so is to import historical preoccupations through the semi-permeable membrane of current interactions. We thereby keep ourselves lodged firmly in a fixed image and role of 'me', and disengaged from those with whom we are interacting.

The interpersonal sense of symptoms

A symptom is a deviation from well-being. In the interpersonal perspective however it is also part of the structure of interaction. Symptoms are the matters of which the client complains, the reasons for coming to therapy, the stimulus to change. They take many forms according to the sufferer's own sense of well-being.

A person suffers from a symptom. The word means something that 'just happens', that befalls one. There are several implications of this apparently unproblematic notion.

The voice of symptoms

Part of Freud's work was to show that symptoms do not just happen. Although apparently senseless, and not immediately understandable, they speak a language. They are part of a language-like discourse with other people. They do not just have physiological causes. They are meaningful responses to what has happened in the person's life.

So what does happen to produce symptoms? Much of the distress in our world does indeed just happen, and many of the happenings are social. Any individual is cast into this life, and is caught up in its movement, taking her experience from participation in it. She might be born clever or handicapped, in a prosperous society or among refugees, black or white, middle-class or working-class. As far as she is concerned the family she enters, and her scope for interaction or choice, just befall her.

Many symptoms, and most of the symptoms discussed in this book, are a consequence of the ways in which we organize our society. Serious depression, for instance, affects some 30 per cent of women in inner London during any one year (Brown and Harris, 1978). Depression is unequally distributed: men, country-dwellers, the middle classes, suffer less than women, particularly married women, people living in inner cities and the working classes. Threatening life events like serious losses and disappointments provoke depression, and they occur universally. But the social resources of community, family, confidants, friends, employment and opportunities for social interaction are distributed most unequally in our society. These resources can befall one according to one's birth and talents. Brown and Harris have shown how it is precisely the lack of these resources that transform losses and disappointments into hopeless and long-lasting despair, into symptoms of depression.

Symptoms of depression and anxiety are twice as common in women as in men in urban western society. Alcoholism and criminality are very much more common in men than women. One could imagine that more women internalize their conflicts, and more men act them out. Men moreover have ways of enacting the discrepancies of society in institutionalized violence such as war and economic exploitation which are hidden behind façades of apparent rationality. We each apparently have a distinctive way of expressing the impossibility of contradictory demands we feel are placed on us in our participation in life.

Psychiatry tends to see psychiatric symptoms as senseless and irrational, as malfunctions to be relieved, calmed, removed or in any case stopped (see for instance a psychiatry textbook such as Slater and Roth, 1977, and also a critique of this response for example Ingleby, 1981). But the therapist's view is different. It is to take symptoms seriously. When one does this one hears of disappointment, of disapproval and of disqualification, which the person concerned has no real way of dealing with. What has happened is as Mead said, that relationships in the external world have been internalized and then form the basis for subsequent experience and relating. Fortunately the person's liveliness is not extinguished by the experience of feeling, and often of being, powerless in the face of adversity. But as one might expect from the powerless, the voice is disguised, and subversive rather than direct. It is as if when living in an occupied territory, symptoms act as the non-co-operation and sabotage of the underground resistance movement. They are the disquieting eruptions that form the antithesis to some of the circumstances of the way we live.

The symptoms that therapists meet include states of alienation, of involuntary actions, emotions and thoughts.

Part of the purpose of therapy is to allow the symptom, where it is an internalized transformation of some previously external contradiction, to speak effectively, rather than ineffectively. Where a symptom is unintelligible, and therefore involuntary or alien, the purpose of therapy is to allow it to become intelligible, so that it can be owned. The transformation sought in therapy is from impotence to effectiveness, or to potency as Freudians would have it.

It goes without saying that the main response to the symptoms arising in our society must be political. We need to find better ways of living together, better ways of distributing resources, of arranging community. Therapy is an adjunct to this aim: not to provide calming or adjustment, but to help articulate the voice of symptoms and allow it to be effective, rather than to be a sabotage of self at the same time that it complains.

So symptoms, as well as arising out of our participation in society, speak back. But their voice is ambiguous. It might turn out that complaints become direct and effective rather than hidden. It might also turn out that some of the underground frustration and rage might turn to gratitude, forgiveness or acceptance as we realize that parents, perhaps, were good as well as being unsatisfactory in some ways, not to be split into pieces; and that our strategies, chosen to deal with the unsatisfactory aspects, also influenced what went on.

Complaints

The voice of symptoms makes sense in a number of ways. First, as a complainant, the sufferer attempts to engage the other in doing something about the problem, redressing it, helping her put right what has gone wrong. The other person is invited into a complementary relationship of helper to this helpless person. It is possible that this other might be able to do something, as a mother was once able to do something to comfort a child – but when, as is often the case, the complaints are about wrongs sustained long ago, the other can be left in the position of feeling as helpless as the person who complains.

This effect is just one transformation of not being able to participate in the current interaction. A complaint is no doubt about a keen unhappiness. But the complaining and the inability to see that the person being complained to is not the image who haunts one from the past, not the person who could possibly redress the wrong, makes things worse, and compounds the sorrow with the other's non-responsiveness. The patient in the mental hospital asking for the salt could only realistically expect the salt to be passed. The others there could realistically only take part in the activity of sharing a meal, and could not bind up whatever wound the depressed patient felt, and made so effectively present with his lugubrious tone.

Preoccupations, especially sad, impotently angry or frightened ones, can effectively prevent one from taking part in anything that might occur in an interaction. So the distress is amplified. It is not just opting out or flooding out that prevent our participation. More permanent regrets and bitterness may convince us that no interactions are worth taking part in at all. That there is something wrong with whatever we might be doing, that complaining is the only course possible.

Symptoms as tactics

A second interpersonal sense of the symptom is that it is something a person does to someone else. As Haley (1963) puts it: symptoms are tactics in human relations. They can be used to control relationships between people. Just as the child tries to control a disadvantageous proposal by saying, 'All right then I won't play', a symptom is a bid to change the rules of interaction.

Everything we say and do with one another includes an element of confirming, extending, contradicting or changing the rules of a relationship. It has an element of negotiating change in the immediate interpersonal community. Whereas the rules of formal games are moderately fixed, the rules of interactions and of culture cannot be formally specified. They change continually. One way to change the rules of an interaction is to introduce a new element. For instance, instead of just saying 'Hello', someone might say, 'Hello, would you like to come and have a cup of coffee?' For the other to agree endorses having coffee together as part of what can take place in the relationship. It perhaps suggests the possibility too, that further kinds of meeting might follow. Everything we do or say has this negotiatory component. As well as what we say, there is both how we say it, and the implications these matters have for the relationship.

Haley argues that we cannot avoid negotiating our relationships, though we can be unaware that we are doing it. Furthermore, we cannot fail to influence the rules of what goes on. If someone says 'Hello', one does not avoid having an influence by not replying. Not to reply to a greeting is a powerful move in the interpersonal field. It is 'cutting the other person dead'.

Symptoms too are part of the redefinitional moves of a relationship, just as Mirabel made a move by implying he no longer wanted to play cards, but would do so to oblige. Fainall, being sensitive to this interpersonal move, asks Mirabel whether an occurrence in a love affair distracts him from cards. This is indeed the case.

A psychiatric symptom is a much more powerful move than Mirabel's. A symptom is indeed amongst the most powerful interpersonal moves that one can make. Haley's word 'tactic' is not inappropriate, since rather than being a negotiable bid for the relationship to be like this or like that, the symptom both demands a particular kind of response from the other, and at the same time disclaims any responsibility or knowledge of the move having been made. Although if Bateson is right no part can have unilateral control on a system; a symptom is an attempt by someone who feels without any other form of negotiation to exercise unilateral control. It is a desperate measure, implying that the sufferer is in a desperate state.

Ms Cindy S for instance, with her agoraphobic symptoms, suffers from a desperate unconfidence. Her 'me' is fixed in a state of knowing that she is seen by others as easily humiliated, and so she does not risk that by going out. She also needs to keep her husband close at hand. Her heart condition and her anxieties (not she herself) arrange that she cannot be left alone for too long, so that apart from his work her husband spends all his time with her. It is not an entirely satisfactory solution. She might prefer to know that her husband stayed at home because he wanted to be with her. But in relational terms we might imagine that she feels so desperate that she has declined that unpredictable possibility, for the more certain prospect of making sure that he will be there. Perhaps she is so tortured by the possibility that he will turn into her image of the bad threatening other, that he has to be kept as firmly in a compassionate role as possible.

And he does take that role. For just as she is engaged in trying to control, not her husband as such, but the complementary relationship, so too is he. By being available he is beyond the reproach of any anger she might otherwise show. He can also see himself as helpful where she is helpless, strong where she is weak, competent where she is incompetent.

The unspoken rules of their arrangement have some other advantages for him too. Bob is rather prone to jealousy, and with his wife at home he doesn't have to cope with that. Without her heart condition Cindy might have to chance getting a job, or not getting one. And with his wife as independent rather than dependent, who knows what this might do for Bob's sense of himself as husband and provider.

Many marriages are negotiated around complementary structures. It is not that complementarities or roles are in themselves bad. But a symptom is an attempt to force a particular complementarity. It does not negotiate. It demands. One can infer that symptomatic people acquire something deeply important by means of their suffering. They acquire predictability. But for something to be a symptom implies that it has a heavy cost for the sufferer. In the case of Cindy and her husband, the cost is a gross restriction of their lives. Presumably their arrangement together is more important to them than the restrictions of other activities.

But a symptom is a word of hope too, a sign that however fixed a structure of interaction might be, it is worth complaining about. The decision to undertake therapy, which is itself the most important move in the therapeutic endeavour, is a sign of life.

A therapist entering into this field of interpersonal negotiations might make a difference. She might be able to decline the invitation simply to become the complement to the complaints and interpersonal demands of the sufferer. She might herself be able to initiate a change in the habitual pattern of relating.

3

Individuality

People in western culture identify themselves very closely with their feelings: being in love, or bereft, or happy, or angry, or anxious, or sad. Yet why should this be? Such feelings just occur. People seldom have any sense of themselves creating feelings voluntarily. Rather, they are moved by them, as the term 'emotion' suggests.

It is around the fulcrum of feelings that many modern therapies turn: psychoanalysis with its pointing towards disowned loves and hates, humanistic and body-oriented therapies with their slogan of getting in touch with feelings, behavioural therapies with their relearning of conditioned states of feeling, cognitive therapies with the changing of feelings by changing of thoughts. Through all these runs the idea that a healthy person experiences feelings without avoiding or distorting them, that neurosis arises by such distortions, and that more direct experiencing allows fulfilment of who one is.

The therapeutic idea is in part to address the nameless agitations and dreads which build up in a person, the explosions of painful feeling which burst over someone, or the strange lacks of feeling such as emptiness and futility. In naming and owning of such agitations of experience people become themselves.

Human culture did not always encourage the seeing of selves as separate beings moved by emotions, moving towards goals in their motives, and having their own thoughts. Far-Eastern culture, influenced by early writings such as the Lao Tzu, has strains which are sceptical of this interpretation. But western culture coming down via the Mesopotamians, the Greeks and the Hebrews is explicit. People are individuals, separate, responsible for their feelings, thoughts, actions. In European history, cultures emerge where this is the explicit theory. Members of such cultures internalize these ideas and give themselves a sense of individuality.

Jaynes's theory of the origin of consciousness

Perhaps the Greeks of Homer's time offer for westerners the easiest and most informative point of reference, already partly like modern western people, yet in their sense of individuality quite unlike. A vivid contrast emerges between ourselves and this ancient culture as written about in the *Iliad* by Homer nearly three millenia ago.

The stark contrast with the theories of personality held by Homer is that in the culture of the *Iliad* there was no sense of emotions, motives or minds as the possessions of individuals. This is pointed out by Snell (1953) and by Jaynes (1976). Ancient hearers of the *Iliad* presumably were interested in these matters, since the first words of the epic are: 'Of wrath sing, oh goddess', an invocation of the muse to begin the tale of Achilles's anger towards King Agamemnon. Yet strikingly, unlike twentieth-century stories, although there are agitations and motives such as wrath and revenge, they were not thought of as attributes of individuals. The wrath around which the story turns doesn't really come from Achilles, who experiences it. It is the anger of a god ricocheting around among the leaders of the Greek army. 'Which of the gods set them to fight against one another?' asks the eighth line of the poem. It was the god Apollo.

Jaynes argues that the *Iliad* documents the dawning of European consciousness. Of the terms used today for thinking about individual selves – emotions, motives, mind – none appears in modern form in the *Iliad*. Agitations and disturbances there are aplenty, but these are bodily sensations, agitations of breathing, of pounding heart, of churning guts. Motives there are too; but many of the main motives come from gods, as very often do thoughts, realizations and plans. To modern people the most peculiar aspect is that there is no concept at all of mind or individual selfhood.

So as Jaynes points out, here are people acting quite recognizably, yet they seemingly have no sense of self. They are not conscious as modern western culture understands the term.

One of the striking (and questionable) ideas of Jaynes is that where Homer wrote that Achilles or some other mortal heard the voice of a god or goddess speaking to him, exactly that was meant: Achilles was hallucinated; perhaps like a modern schizophrenic commanded by authoritative voices, or experiencing thoughts or feelings put into him from outside. Rather than speaking as many people now do, of voices inside their heads, of inner debate or of knowing what they feel, these ancient people simply experienced thoughts coming to them, feelings as agitations of the body, motives as directives from gods, thoughts as being given to them.

It's not such a bad theory. People today do not really know how they compose the words they speak, do not actually experience themselves making thoughts out of some mental substance, do not experience themselves generating feelings, or creating motives. Mental events occur. They just come. They show themselves. How they emerge is unbeknownst to any individual. Unbeknownst is perhaps a better translation of Freud's term usually translated as 'unconscious'. For the Greeks the idea that mental events came from gods was a theory by which they experienced their world, just as in the twentieth century people have a theory that they themselves create such mental events (Oatley, 1981a), or that they have minds inside which things happen.

There are six words which are common in the *Iliad*, and which Jaynes says are translated anachronistically in modern versions, as mental terms. However, he argues, in the *Iliad* there are no terms that actually refer to mental events. The terms that are translated as mental refer only to bodily matters. *Thumos* is the commonest. Properly speaking in the *Iliad* it means simply 'activity' – being killed stops it. It can also mean agitation or disturbance. In modern physiological terms it is activation of the sympathetic division of the autonomic nervous system such as is occasioned by excitement, anger or fright. It is often not the warrior who wants to fight, or who rejoices but his *thumos*. Next commonest is the term *phrenes*. This means 'lungs' or breathing. People's breathing changes nowadays, when some change of feeling occurs, either very obviously as when laughing or sobbing, but also when alerted or drowsing. *Kradie* is a term still in our mental vocabulary. It means 'heart', and people now speak as if they felt certain emotions, particularly love, in the heart. In the *Iliad* what is referred to is a pounding of the heart. Last of these psychosomatic terms is *etor* meaning 'guts' which are sometimes spilled over the field of battle, or which churn or cramp, or nauseate.

The two other proto-mental terms that Jaynes says are used by Homer are *noos* and *psyche*, the one surviving in the old-fashioned slang term 'nous' meaning intelligence, and the other of course in terms like psychology – the forerunner of the modern notion of mind. In the *Iliad* though, *noos* means 'sight' or gaze, so Zeus keeps Hector in his *noos*, keeps him in sight. But still, insists Jaynes, 'No one makes any decisions in his "*noos*".' Similarly *psyche* does not mean 'mind' in the way western people use it. Rather it is like *thumos* almost synonymous with the notion of being alive, or 'livingness'. It can be taken away by a spear in the right place, or coughed out, or it may simply leave. As Jaynes points out, except in one passage in the *Iliad* which scholars agree is a later interpolation in which *psyche* refers to what might remain after death, *psyche* is used only to mean livingness. In the *Iliad*, says Jaynes, 'No one in any way ever sees, decides, thinks, knows, fears or remembers anything in his psyche' (p. 271).

So here were people whose theory, and language for talking about themselves and their experience, was radically different from today's. They had no terms for mental states, or conscious decision-making as such. The terms which later became mental terms did not imply consciousness in the *Iliad*. In the first four of them we can recognize the targets of modern psychosomatic illness – *thumos*, *phrenes*, *kradie*, *etor* – in panic attacks, asthma, cardiac conditions, duodenal ulcers. The other two, *noos* and *psyche*, now meaning 'intelligence' and 'mind', were used to mean 'sight' and 'livingness'. In the earliest Greek writing no thoughts or feelings occurred in them.

Jaynes's theory of the coming of individual consciousness as

33

western people now understand it is that beginning soon after the time described in the *Iliad* people began to think, act, feel, will for themselves, and not under the direction of voices of gods that came to them in times of stress. When they did so, they started to suppose that thoughts and so forth occurred in a kind of metaphorical space, which we now call 'mind'. Now people talk of mind as an entity like a container or a space, and ideas as entities which can be inside or outside that container: 'I'll keep you in mind for the job.' Feelings too are entities, though their location is less often described except in limited cases such as, 'My heart is full of love for you.' The self too exists in space, and there is an inside and an outside. Feelings are entities, substances, to be kept in, kept under control, or let out, expressed. Decisions take place in containers which people own: 'I wasn't really sure in my own mind what to do for the best.' These aren't just changes of words. They are changes in concepts, changes in behaviour, changes in history. Ancient writing is a kind of archaeological site with its broken potsherds, from remains of which can be reconstructed something of a past culture, so that we can understand as Jaynes says the 'broken off bits of vocabulary . . . that came next to refer to some kind of mental function' (p. 292).

The Greeks had ideas of madness in terms of their cultural norms (see for example Simon, 1978). But for us, living as it were inside a different theory of identity, it is deviations from what we now take to be an individual, autonomous identity which are felt as psychiatric distress. Our newer definition of selfhood seems more restrictive than the Greek one, and we tend to experience many influences 'outside' our own agency as being disturbing. What we define as psychiatric illness might indeed more properly be called a disturbance of the modern sense of individuality and autonomy of the self. Foulds (1965, 1976) has made just a set of definitions.

Foulds's hierarchy of personal illness

In formulating his diagnostic scheme, Foulds has abandoned the scheme of psychiatric textbooks, that symptoms are like the symptoms of physical disease which fall into clusters because they are characteristic malfunctions caused by a particular pathological agent.

He makes a distinction between personality and symptoms.

34

Personality is a long-standing patterning of behaviour, and symptoms are differences from the usual. He then defines realms of behaviour unacceptable to self or to others, and attributable to personality or to more temporary symptoms. Behaviour distressing to others but not to self tends to be labelled 'crime' in western society. The symptomatic disturbs both self and others, and it is this that constitutes personal illness – the major concern of both therapists and psychiatrists.

For Foulds, illness has a hierarchical structure of increasing disintegration of the sense of an autonomous self. The lowest level of illness he calls dysthymic states. The word 'dysthymic' is derived from the Homeric Greek *thumos*. 'Dysthymic' might be translated as distressingly disturbed or discouraged. In the more usual psychiatric terminology these states include panics, despairs and the like.

Ms Cindy S clearly suffers from these dysthymic disturbances. When she is in such a state she can scarcely act. She is compelled, and all volition is removed from her. But it is temporary. Afterwards she feels her old self.

At the next level of the hierarchy are states which will include dysthymic states, but will also have some well-established neurotic condition such as a phobia, an obsessional compulsive disorder such as having to spend several hours a day washing the hands, or a psychosomatic illness like asthma or eczema.

Cindy's disturbance also occurs at this level of Foulds's hierarchy. In the traditional language of psychiatry she has a phobia: agoraphobia.

The third class, which includes symptoms of the lower levels, Foulds calls an integrated delusion, for instance a delusion of grandeur or persecution or of contrition.

Occasionally Cindy also feels oppressed by this level of disturbance, though usually it is more within bounds. But when she is out sometimes, she has had overwhelming convictions that men are looking at her with intentions to humiliate her.

At the highest level are disintegrated delusions, which involve hallucinations, experiences of having one's thoughts put into one or taken away, of oneself being not alive but a machine, or of being dead: in other words of scarcely having a self at all.

So according to Foulds, to suffer a personal illness is to lose some or all sense of one's individuality or selfhood. Many people have symptoms which are manageable. It is when they become intense or prolonged and unmanageable for the self or others, that we speak of a breakdown having happened. The person can no longer cope.

Movement up the hierarchy corresponds to progressive depersonalization. At lower levels one might be disturbed some of the time but have a sense of oneself as being disturbed. At the highest level one has a very disintegrated sense of self or none at all. Integrated selfhood corresponds to the voluntary, the individually autonomous, and its loss to being taken over partly or wholly by something alien.

Freud's science of mind

More than any other person, it was Freud who ushered in the modern era of thinking about ourselves and the deviations from individual selfhood to which therapists attend. Descartes (1637) in his famous phrase 'I think therefore I am' (p. 53) had implied the identity of selfhood with the voluntary, conscious agent. It remained to Descartes's followers (see Whyte, 1978) including Freud to enunciate the further and disturbing implication of this. That which we feel or do involuntarily has not gone away. It is present, making itself felt, but unconscious.

It was into a world where people had individual selves, had feelings, thought things in their minds, acted, and decided, that Freud came. But psychoanalysis also began a new language for discussing mental events, and gave new names to the involuntary agitations and disturbances that individuals experienced. It gave also the idea of 'interpretation'; that by exploring the individual mind, and naming archaic wishes and feelings, the person would be freed from the transformation of these disturbances into symptoms.

Freud's work is fundamental for the understanding of psychotherapeutic practice, ranging from the behavioural to the humanistic. Just as Homer provides a source for the transition into a recognizable culture of urban civilization peopled by selves, so Freud's writings provide a source for understanding the psychological transformation into the twentieth century.

This is not the place for an exposition of Freud's ideas and practice. Rather just one aspect of his work will be discussed, his therapeutic naming of the agitations and disturbances which are experienced by the modern self.

The phenomena on which Freud concentrated, which people experience as happening, rather than as being willed by themselves, include the free associations of therapy, dreams, slips of the tongue and other mistakes, symptoms, and the bodily states of changed heartbeat, breathing or gut-churning described by Homer.

Symptoms are those events which 'just happen', but which a person, or those to whom that person is related, find distressing. At a further level of distress, when such symptoms became intolerable, medical or psychotherapeutic help is sought.

One can note that not just states of distress but states of delight are experienced as losing oneself. So one can lose oneself in a play, a novel, a film, some music; one can lose oneself in a game or an intense conversation. One can lose oneself by being in love. So evidently to be healthy or hale implies a subtle relationship between the voluntary and involuntary. The search for 'the wholeness of being human' which is therapy is certainly not the simple matter of abolishing the involuntary.

Much though the different schools of psychotherapy like to assert their differences from one another it is to this mystery, the complex and sometimes paradoxical relation of the voluntary to the involuntary, of competence in carrying out plans to the acceptance of what just happens, that they devote themselves.

Freud's theory of the involuntary

Part of Freud's achievement was to array madness and mental symptomatology on the spectrum of recognizable human experience. He did this by bringing into focus the irrational, the involuntary, the unconscious, in everyone. So against the prevailing current of rationalism which suppresses the irrational, the out-of-control, he drew attention to the common underlying structure of parapraxes, dreams, symptoms.

Parapraxes are, in the words of the subtitle of *The Psychopathology of Everyday Life* (1901), those events of 'forgetting, slips of the tongue, bungled actions, superstitions and errors' that we are aware of as not really being ourselves. They are the minor intrusions of the involuntary into those aspects of everyday life

37

which are generally thought to be voluntary. As an example of Freud's treatment of such matters here is the 'aliquis' case from his 1901 book (p. 46–9).

The 'aliquis' case

Freud on holiday meets a young man he knows. In the course of conversation on the plight of the Jews the young man starts out to quote a line of Virgil but cannot get the line right because he has forgotten the apparently insignificant word *aliquis*, meaning 'someone'. Freud, fortunately also familiar with Virgil, supplies the word, and the two fall to discussing how such lapses of memory occur. Freud, in his now famous injunction, to 'free-associate', the only rule of psychoanalytic therapy, enjoins the young man, 'Tell me *candidly* and *uncritically* whatever comes into your mind if you direct your attention to the forgotten word without any definite aim.' He asks the young man to allow himself to be taken over by the thoughts and images that occur involuntarily.

The young man does so, and says that for no apparent reason the word divides into two: 'a' and 'liquis'. With Freud's encouragement he finds 'relics' and 'liquid' coming to mind, puns of the second part. He talks of relics he had recently seen, of the accusation of ritual blood sacrifice which was being brought against the Jews, a subject that Freud reminds him is not unrelated to the subject of the 'social status of the race to which we both belonged' that they had been discussing. The young man then talks about an article he has read about St Augustine's views on women. Under Freud's prompting further saints come to mind: 'Now it's St Januarius and the miracle of his blood that comes to mind – my thoughts seem to me to be running on mechanically', he says. Freud asks him to talk about the miracle, and he recounts how the blood kept in a phial miraculously liquefies on a certain day, and that he remembered a story of Garibaldi waiting for a sign that might encourage his troops, who '*hoped* the miracle would take place soon'.

'Why do you pause?' asks Freud. The young man protests that something too intimate has come to mind. But Freud has guessed. So the young man says, 'I've suddenly thought of a lady from whom I might easily hear a piece of news that would be very awkward for us.' And Freud supplies the connection, 'That her periods have stopped', together with the linking ideas of calendar saints named after months, that blood starts to flow on a particular day, and so on.

Evidently, writes Freud, the young man was trying to keep this unwelcome subject out of mind. In keeping it out of mind, the mechanisms of association also kept out of mind the apparently harmless word 'aliquis' as well. But what people try to suppress 'always tries to assert itself elsewhere, but is successful only when suitable conditions meet it half way' (p. 42). These conditions quite often occur, as in the chance association between his waiting for his friend's period, and Garibaldi's waiting for the miracle of the flowing of the blood. It is possible that in his conversation, the young man might have been struck by a sudden pang of realizing his preoccupation. This was not what occurred. It was a more oblique hint at the preoccupation, though just as disturbing to the conversation.

Dream interpretation

Freud treated dreams in the same way. Preoccupations, or as he calls them 'wishes', surface in forms that are often disguised. Here is an example from Freud's *Introductory Lectures* (1916–17).

> A lady who though she was still quite young, had been married for many years, had the following dream: She was at the theatre with her husband. One side of the stalls was completely empty. Her husband had told her that Elise L and her fiancé had wanted to go too, but had only been able to get bad seats – three for one florin 50 kreuzers. (pp. 153–6)

By asking the dreamer for associations Freud learned that the dream was touched off by hearing of the friend Elise L's engagement, and of another event in which the dreamer had booked so early for a play that she had wanted to see, that she had incurred a booking fee, though when she went, one side of the stalls was almost empty. Her husband teased her for having been in too much of a hurry. The lady could find no association to the idea of three seats for two people, but Freud guesses that it was an allusion to Elise being only three months younger than her. The 1 Fl 50 brought the association of her sister-in-law having been given a present of 150 florins by her husband. She 'had been in a great hurry – the silly goose – to rush off to the jewellers' and exchange the money for a piece of jewellery.'

With not much more ado, Freud gets the sense that the dream is about being in too much of a hurry. What the dreamer had been in too much of a hurry to do was to get married. This feeling had been given a resentment-provoking prod by her husband telling her of the engagement of Elise who was only three months younger than herself, to a particularly eligible man. If she'd not been in so much of a hurry to get married, she might have got someone a hundred times better, just as the 150 florins were a hundred times better than the price of three theatre tickets.

Symptoms

Symptoms too, argued Freud, have the same underlying manner of creation – only they are larger and more troublesome than the discontinuities of a conversation or the disguised but largely harmless intrusion of disturbing preoccupations into dreams.

The clinical psychologist who saw Ms Cindy S was not psychoanalytically oriented, but a psychoanalytic perspective can be constructed from some of the case notes. Had Cindy been seeing a psychoanalytic therapist meanings of the following kind might have started to occur between them. Though 25, Cindy was committed to being a teenager. To venture into the world at all she had to have either her actual parent with her, or some-one who behaved like a parent. Only then was her heart at ease.

Her relationships with men also had something to do with her symptoms. There had been only two kinds of men in her world, men who were cruel and perhaps lecherous, and men who were kindly and supportive, but also who could easily be taken in. Her husband while mostly seen as the second kind could occasionally seem very threatening if he acted unkindly, when she could start feeling terrified, having palpitations and other psychosomatic symptoms. On occasions when this had occurred she had gone to be looked after by her mother.

Going out was replete with sexual innuendo, and she found it difficult not to think continually that men on the street might molest her, or else think she looked stupid. When with her husband, much of their conversation inside the safety of their car was to comment scornfully on the men they saw, how stupid they were, how gross, and so on.

A psychoanalytic therapist might see that an issue of therapy would be Cindy's dependency, which she could not do without but also resented; and the impotence of being unable to act in the world except through the intermediary of her husband or mother. In getting them to do things for her though, she felt sure they saw her as a drip, which she hated and despaired of.

Though owning such painful meanings as these in her quest to rediscover her autonomy, Cindy at the start of therapy had only the haziest sense of connections of this kind, or that her symptoms had a strategic quality in her relations with others (cf. Haley, 1963; Ryle, 1982). Mostly she felt oppressed by involuntary intrusions into her life: her heart condition, being housebound and being taken over by moods and terrors over which she had no control.

For Freud all these incongruities of the involuntary intruding into the carefully maintained structure of rationality and polite demeanour are generated by ideas activating one another in sequences of association. And like a truly western thinker in the manner described by Jaynes, Freud explained the mind as a kind of space in the head, like a room, in which thoughts, wishes, affects might occur, or from which they might be expelled. So when a thought is in mind it is conscious, but when it is not then it is unconscious, but still present.

These unconscious time-bombs, ready to explode and disrupt the surface of social selfhood, are produced by the same mechanism: a wish or a strong feeling, which we feel that if pursued, would have devastating consequences. Freud's young friend telling of his woman friend perhaps being pregnant might win Freud's disapproval. The wish of the woman of the theatre dream to have a more socially advantageous husband threatens the idea that one, of course, loves one's husband. Cindy's heart condition keeps at bay the even more terrifying possibility that she might have to take her chances in the world.

Condensation and displacement

By repressing something and keeping it out of mind space, it remains a nameless danger, an anxiety, ever ready to return in disguised form. The mechanisms of mind construct the disguise.

They merge ideas together, in what Freud called 'condensation'. So the word 'aliquis' becomes the single representative of several trains of ideas, the node at which these strings of associations cross. At the same time a second mechanism called 'displacement' substitutes forgetting a word for wanting to forget about his woman friend's period being due. More seriously for Cindy, her heart condition becomes the representative of several of her trains of wishes and ideas, allowing her to avoid having to confront strange men, or the uncertainties of the outside world, and simultaneously making her husband into a slave. A displacement of responsibility for this occurs: it's not her who does this, but her heart complaint, which just happens.

Condensation is an intersection of several associative pathways, displacement is the substitution of an inappropriate terminal for a charge of psychical energy travelling along an associative pathway. Because of the translations wrought by these two processes people are unable to recognize the significance of some things they think and do. Their actions, thoughts, feelings, become unrecognizable, alien, unconscious. Nevertheless they intrude.

So for Freud therapy was the tracing of associations to their intersections and proper terminals, so that a sense of what the original and undisguised feelings and desires were might emerge. By readmitting them to consciousness, they would again become the person's own: the person's self rather than a symptom of not-self.

Such thoughts or feelings need not be blurted out. There are many occasions on which to do that would be most inappropriate. But they could be admitted to consciousness, so that the person might decide, rather than just act without being able to do anything different.

Therapy was conducted by Freud to allow the readmission and reowning of just those impulses and ideas which were themselves struggling anonymously into the open. So Freud's young friend was in the end able to say, 'I'm worried that my woman friend might be pregnant', or the woman of the dream about the theatre might be able to admit to herself, 'I feel my marriage was a mistake – I could have married more advantageously.' Cindy might be able to admit to herself, and perhaps even say to Bob: 'I feel furious and let down at the treachery of men, including you, and I'll do everything I can to make sure you don't leave me.' And in that moment the symptom loses some of its alienating power.

For Freud as for Jaynes to be whole is to be able to admit a thought, an idea, a feeling into the space of consciousness, and make one's own decisions. So the transition from prehistory into history, in the cultural and the personal sense, is the acquisition of this space. As Jaynes points out, Homer's words that meant agitation, and disturbances of breathing, of heartbeat, and of the guts, and the words *noos* and *psyche* meaning sight and livingness, became container metaphors within the next few hundred years of Greek literature. So, according to Jaynes, in Hesiod, writing in the seventh century, there is talk of putting information and advice into *thumos* and *phrenes* as if they were cupboards. By the sixth century *noos* becomes the major word for mind and the famous maxim 'Know thyself' comes to have a meaning it could never have had in Homer, in which for a person who 'has a mind-space called a *noos* in which an analog of himself can narratize out what is . . . right to do' (1976, p. 287). The voices of gods become redundant. During the next few hundred years people become autonomous, individual agents.

Into this tradition too stepped Freud, to gather up those more troublesome aspects of self, the disowned parts – mistakes, lapses, symptoms, until these too can be admitted to the space of mind: owned, admitted to consciousness, so that people might know themselves. These new selves, however, are not the comfortable rational creatures of the enlightenment, rather as Lacan (1966) asserts we enter into a continual unknowability. Such disturbances of the surface of life can never be fully predicted or controlled.

4

The practice of psychotherapy

The many different forms of therapy (see for example Kovel, 1976; Herink, 1980) allow the possibility of trying to discern what common elements they all may have. The major common element is that therapy takes place in a human relationship. This raises the question of constructing a theory of therapeutic practice, based on the relationship between client and therapist. In this chapter, therefore, the nature of this common element, the therapeutic relationship, will be discussed.

One aspect of 'technique' is, however, profoundly important in the therapeutic relationship. It is whether the therapist makes suggestions to the client or not. In this chapter the range of therapies will be divided into two kinds, directive and non-directive.

In directive therapies the therapist gives firm suggestions and advice. In non-directive therapies few suggestions are made. Instead the therapist and client concentrate on making sense of what is going on in the relationship between them, and on understanding the meanings of the client's experience.

In this chapter, one directive therapy (cognitive-behavioural) and one non-directive therapy (psychoanalytic) will be examined, with a view to discovering the relational issues involved in each.

Directive therapy

First Ms Cindy S will be portrayed visiting her therapist, who practises directively, in a cognitive behavioural style, which is perhaps the most common for clinical psychologists working in the British National Health Service at present. Cindy has persuaded her husband to come with her to the clinic, and to wait for her. His work allows him to arrange his time flexibly to some extent.

She walks into the therapist's room, considerably agitated, and is asked to sit in a comfortable chair opposite the therapist, who sits in a similar chair.

The therapist says, 'Your doctor has written to me saying you find it difficult to go out on your own, and that you would like to have some therapy to help cope with some of those problems. Would you like to tell me what the problems are?'

Cindy tells the therapist about her difficulties, about how her heart stops her doing very much, about how she wants to get a job, and needs to be able to get out on her own.

The therapist says, 'You look quite anxious now. It must have taken some courage to come to see me.'

Cindy says that her husband brought her in the car, but that she does feel quite anxious.

Cognitive behavioural therapy

The therapist says that the situation Cindy finds herself in is quite common, that it is called agoraphobia. The word means 'fear of the market-place', but it is usually a fear of going out. If Cindy would devote herself to therapy, there is a good chance that she would be able to go out on her own within a few months.

The therapist asked Cindy to describe what she felt when her heart started pounding, and discovered that it was not just her heart that was the trouble. She felt sick, felt she was going to collapse and felt her mind was blank.

The therapist explained that what Cindy was suffering was a

panic attack. It was a normal bodily reaction of fear, but triggered off in situations where there probably was nothing objectively to be frightened of. She next asked Cindy whether she could go out at all, and what kinds of things she could do with perhaps just a bit of anxiety, but without feeling a complete panic.

'Perhaps I could go to the post-box when there are no people about.'

'What kinds of things would be most difficult to do?'

'Go on a train or an aeroplane. Bob, my husband, wanted to go abroad for a holiday, but I just couldn't.'

The therapist decided to treat Cindy by giving her a graded series of activities to do (Mathews *et al.*, 1981). She explained that the best way to cope with the phobia was to go out to the places that frightened her, but to do it a little at a time, building up confidence as she did so. Next week they would draw up a list of tasks, starting with things that would make her a bit anxious, and moving on to things that she couldn't imagine she would ever be able to do. Starting with the easiest one, Cindy would do one activity a day and then move on to the next most difficult one. She would start with going to her front gate, then to the post-box, then perhaps walking down to a nearby park, and so on.

Relaxation training

The therapist told Cindy that she would give her a way of coping with her anxiety when it started to rise, so that she would be able to do these activities. She said it was not possible just to control panic voluntarily. Instead she had to practise an opposite response, relaxation. After she had practised the relaxation exercise, she would find that by saying the word 'relax' to herself, and relaxing as in the exercise, any anxiety she felt would go down.

She asked Cindy if she had a cassette player at home. She had, so the therapist said she would give her a cassette which contained the relaxation exercise.

The therapist took her through the exercise, which was one of the first procedures introduced into behavioural therapy (Wolpe, 1958). She asked Cindy to sit comfortably and close her eyes. Then going systematically through the body, asked her first to tighten up and then relax each group of muscles in turn. She started with the hands.

'Breathe in, tighten all the muscles of your hands up, into a fist
. . . tight as you can . . . hold it there. Now breathe out. Let the
tension out of your hands, and as you do so say to yourself "relax".
Notice the difference between your hands now when they are
relaxed and when they were tense.'

The exercise repeated tensing and relaxing the hands, moved
on to the forearms, the upper arms, the shoulders and so on until
the whole body had been covered systematically. The exercise
took about half an hour. Cindy was to do it twice a day while
listening to the tape in order to be ready to go out after the next
session.

Cindy was relieved that the therapist had been sympathetic, and
excited that she would be able to do the things that she could not
do at the moment. She felt impatient to start the relaxation
exercises, and even more impatient that she couldn't start the real
thing until next week.

Therapy in progress

At her next session Cindy said she had tried to practise relaxation,
but it hadn't been any good. She had lost patience. She wouldn't
be able to relax in that way; she needed to do things quickly.
Relaxation was just too slow. But she was ready to start doing the
going-out exercises.

The therapist decided to go along with this, though she felt it
was a bad sign that Cindy had not done the first thing she had
suggested.

They drew up a list of progressively more difficult activities
together: going to the front gate and looking up and down the
road, but not going in till she felt calm, going to the post-box,
walking round the block, going into a local newsagent's shop to
buy something, and so on. At the end of the list were items such as
going on a bus to the large supermarket in the middle of town at a
time when it would be crowded, going to buy a cup of tea in a café,
applying for jobs.

For next week, she just had to do the first two activities, going to
the front gate once a day for three days, then the same with going
to the post-box on three days. Cindy said she would be all right
without the relaxation exercise. The therapist told her that if she
did start to feel panicky, she was to tell herself, 'This is just my

body reacting, if I don't wind myself up it will just subside on its own.' Then she should just wait till the anxiety went down, and slowly get on with the activity. The most important thing was not to go back indoors until her anxiety had gone down. The reason she was housebound now was that she had always gone indoors where she felt safe, and her body had learned this. She had to let her body learn that her anxiety would go down on its own when she was out, and then as she practised more it would gradually fade to manage-able proportions.

The following week Cindy came in exuberantly. She said she hadn't started the activities straight away, in fact not till yesterday. In any case she thought that the ones like standing at the front gate or going to the post-box were too easy. But yesterday she had walked to the park, not once but twice. The first time things felt just as bad as she had expected, and she hurried, to get it over with. But when she got back to her house, she remembered she should not go back inside if she was still feeling anxious, and that the anxiety would subside if she didn't wind herself up. She felt determined not to give up, so she decided to go to the park again. 'And do you know,' she said, 'when I was down there, I heard the birds singing.'

The therapist was touched by this incident. She encouraged Cindy to promise to do something every day during the next week, explained further about talking to herself when she started feeling panicky and saying the sorts of things she had said to herself after the first trip to the park: 'It's difficult, but I can do it', 'I will just think about what I am doing now, and not worry about whether I'll be able to do it again tomorrow.'

A setback

The next session Cindy missed. The therapist phoned up later in the day. The phone was answered by Cindy's husband Bob, who said Cindy had had a particularly bad turn. Her heart condition had come on and she had nearly lost consciousness. It was brought on by going to the local newsagent's shop. It had obviously been too much for her and set her heart off. She wasn't strong enough to be going out. The doctor had been called, and Cindy had been in bed for the last three days, resting.

The therapist asked to speak to her, and said that she was sorry to hear that she had been ill. There often were setbacks, but it was important not to give up. She thought that if she took things gently and did a little at a time, she would still be able to go out. She arranged an appointment for the following week.

Somewhat to the therapist's surprise, Cindy did come next week. She had got her mother to bring her this time. She said she wanted to continue. The therapist decided that she needed to encourage Cindy that despite her impatience, she should take things more slowly. Perhaps she had brought her heart condition on by trying to rush things too much. Again somewhat to the therapist's surprise, Cindy agreed. She started to tell the therapist that the reason going out was so difficult was that she hated the idea that men would be looking at her. She felt that they would think she looked stupid, and that if there was someone standing at the end of the street, when she went out of the door, then she would not be able to go in that direction, but would go the other way, and pray that she wouldn't pass anyone.

Upsetting thoughts

The therapist decided that as well as encouraging her to go out, she would ask Cindy to keep a record of upsetting thoughts like 'Oh there's a man over there, he will stare at me', to write these down and to collect as many as she could for next week.

Next week Cindy went out on several days, and collected quite a few thoughts. 'That man will think my hair looks stupid like this . . . If I walk near him he will stare at my legs . . . I don't want to go near him . . . I'll cross to the other side of the road . . . Then he'll notice that I am doing that and think that I am stupid.'

She said that she felt better at being able to trap these thoughts, and knowing that she was going to write them down when she got home made them less frightening.

From this point she started to improve. She came back the next week saying that she had succeeded in going to the local super-market, and that she wanted to practise going on the bus so that she could come to therapy on her own without bothering her mother.

During the next week she had planned to try taking a short bus trip, of two stops, and then to walk home. She had gone out at the right time for the bus, but it had not come. She waited, getting more and more agitated, and then went home, thinking that if she waited any longer she would be late for her mother who had arranged to call round. She recounted how she had felt very depressed later that day, and been unable to get up next morning, feeling in despair and that none of her efforts was worth it. She found herself saying to herself, 'I'd got ready to go on the bus today . . . I managed to get out there . . . I'll never manage it again . . . How feeble and stupid, not even being able to get on a bus.'

As Beck (1976) has pointed out, thought patterns such as these do indeed lead to conclusions that are dreadful: 'I'm stupid . . . I'm feeble . . . I can't even get on a bus . . . If I can't even do that I might just as well not be alive.' They have the consequence that the person reaches the end of these trains of thought feeling quite appropriately to their conclusion – useless, incapable, worthless.

Beck describes these thought patterns as 'automatic'. They are not attended to consciously. As Mead has said, although the voices of these automatic thoughts are importations of the social relationships of childhood, by adulthood the original imagery, perhaps of scathing parental commentary, has faded. Only 'the barely necessary cues' (Mead, 1913, p. 147) now trigger off these thought patterns. For instance, something not going right triggers off a train of self-punishing thoughts and images, which are usually just at the threshold of awareness, but nevertheless their conclusions, which by adulthood have the quality of self-evident truths, are the ones which are powerfully responsible for leaving us feeling panicky, despairing, wretched or defeated.

For many people states of feeling such as these just seem to happen. Cognitive therapists such as Beck (1976) and Ryle (1982) suggest that such people should pay attention to their barely noticeable automatic thought patterns. When they do so, the thoughts become more distinct. They can perhaps write down the sequences of words or images that come to mind, and the situations in which they occur. They often then discover that their moods do not happen for no reason, but follow from the conclusions their disattended automatic thought patterns lead them to, and are related to situations or ideas that act as cues to trigger them off. By paying attention to these thoughts, the person can reown them, and reconsider in a more reflective way that the rules of her life need no longer decree that she is about to be humiliated because there is a man on the street corner, or useless because a

bus fails to arrive, although it is indeed depressing to feel humiliated or useless.

With her therapist's encouragement, Cindy continued to record her frightening thought patterns, and the next week succeeded in taking a bus ride on her own.

Relational aspects of a directive therapy

Ms Cindy S's main complaint was that she could not go out, and
that what prevented her from doing so was her heart condition.
Her panics were of such intolerable proportions that she felt that
something nameless and dreadful was about to happen. As well as
her pounding heart, she felt faint, felt a heaving of the guts, and
her mind going blank except for the idea of escaping: the gamut of
psychosomatic agitations described in Homer's *Iliad*, proper to
the nearness of death.

The action of a cognitive behaviour therapist is to make
suggestions. The therapist entered Cindy's interpersonal field as
an authoritative figure, offering hope, at a time when Cindy was
feeling particularly oppressed by her symptoms, and was wanting
to do something about them.

Behaviour and cognitive therapists often give an account of
their work as if it is a technical matter. It is as if some piece of
maladaptive learning has gone on, for instance, in agoraphobia,
learning that avoiding going out decreases the likelihood of
anxiety and panic. Perhaps this happens in nervous systems which
are particularly susceptible to stress or anxiety. The technical task
is to have the client unlearn the maladaptive response and learn a
more adaptive one.

In this chapter a different explanation for the success of
cognitive behavioural methods will be given. It is that they occur
within a structure of human relating.

Suggestions and refusals

The therapist using cognitive-behavioural methods is usually
careful, like other therapists, to avoid telling the client how to run
her life. It would be completely useless for the therapist to say to
Cindy, 'You should get out more, and you wouldn't feel so
miserable.' She already knows that, but she cannot. Instead the

therapist suggests first that she does something that she has said she can. Then the therapist leaves the client with the expectation that she will do what she herself has said she will. Temporarily, the client hands over responsibility for her actions to the therapist, who takes responsibility for their effects. It is difficult for Cindy to refuse to do what they have agreed.

Nevertheless, Cindy does refuse. She refuses to do the relaxation exercises, and gives as an excuse that she is too impatient.

Her therapist might have used her authority and said that if Cindy did not do the exercises then she could not treat her. She didn't do this. In interpersonal terms she conceded. She gave in to a kind of symptom, impatience, which was presumably closely related to her anxiety, in the way that Cindy experienced everyone giving in to her symptoms. In Haley's (1963) terms Cindy takes some control of the relationship by this manoeuvre. A complementary structure of 'You suggest – I'll find out why that isn't any good' is instantiated. But the therapist perhaps realizes that this defiance is not just cantankerousness, but the voice of Cindy's own assertion, which therapy will hinge on.

The therapist takes up the client's own suggestion that she can go out without the coping strategy of relaxation. The therapist suggests that the client does exactly what she herself has proposed, and go out without having done the relaxation training.

The possibilities of therapy balance on a knife edge at this point. If this kind of manoeuvre occurred in industrial or international negotiation, it would be called 'brinkmanship'. Cindy avoids doing anything until the day before seeing her therapist, and perhaps knowing that she has to face the therapist's possible relinquishment of concern, and partly because she does also want to do something different, she goes out. What she does has its quantum of defiance (or assertion). Instead of following the gradual programme which they have agreed, she goes straight for a step to be taken a week later, walking to the park.

But in so doing she surprises herself and the therapist. The outside world, which for her was a threatening minefield, became one where she could just be walking along, unworried enough to notice the sound of birdsong. No therapist could advise or suggest this switch, let alone make it happen. A therapist might work with a client to clear some of the ground so that it became more possible, and so that the person's healing potential might be mobilized.

Escalation

Later the same interpersonal drama of suggestion and defiance, accompanied by the convincing reason why nothing else was possible was played out again, in another key and now with full orchestration. While doing an activity suggested by the therapist, Cindy's heart had become 'hyperkinetic'. She entered a medical emergency. Her husband was called. Then the doctor, who gave medication. She took to bed for three days, and missed her appointment. Presumably if the therapist had not got in touch with her Cindy would have convinced herself and her husband that therapy was impossible. Her heart prevented her from being anything but an invalid.

The therapist got a strong sense of all this when she phoned. (And phoning is not what therapists are supposed to do.) Cindy's husband, without actually saying so, let the therapist feel that he thought she had pushed Cindy too far. He made it clear by his tone that he felt that was enough.

However, the therapist did not give up. She asked Cindy to come back for another appointment. Cindy came with her mother. Though cognitive-behaviour therapists would not typically re-mark on this, it seemed that the alliances in Cindy's world had shifted temporarily. Her husband who had backed therapy to start with had now changed his mind. But perhaps because of the phone call, which might have convinced Cindy of her thera-pist's concern, she herself wanted to go on, and recruited her mother.

A working alliance

In the next phase Cindy and the therapist seemed to have formed a working alliance. Cindy was pleased to find not only that she was able to do things that she had formerly not been able to do, like going to the supermarket, but also that she could do them under her own agency. It was she who decided to walk to the park, she who decided to go straight for the supermarket, she who dis-covered that writing down her self-defeating thoughts took away a lot of their power over her.

In relational terms, what the therapist did was to lend her support to actions that seemed impossible. Cindy was assertive, though, as in the way of people not used to having any direct influence, her assertion was defiance disguised as an inability to do anything different. The therapist maintained the implied commitments that Cindy had already made as points of departure, commitments like, 'I can manage without the relaxation exercises, I can walk down to the park.' In so doing the therapist supported that part of Cindy who did want to give up her agoraphobic symptoms, while not negating Cindy's expressions of her independence.

The possibility of starting to give up the role of incompetent had started to affect Cindy's relationship with her husband, which would also have to be negotiated between them. It would mean for instance that he would have to give up the exclusive preserve of the competent, helpful one.

Although interpersonal negotiations occur in any therapy, behaviour and cognitive therapists seldom talk about them. Indeed it would be possible for Cindy's therapist to conduct this whole therapeutic sequence without attending to or even being aware of the interpersonal aspects at all. As far as the therapist was concerned, therapy started with some difficulties, and got going well when she found a mode of working which was suitable for the client, namely having her write down the distressing and self-defeating thoughts, and encouraging her to replace them with more realistic and positive ones.

An attributional analysis of therapy

One way of seeing this, as Totman (1982, 1984) has argued, is in terms of the social psychological theory of attribution, and as a version of the so-called cognitive dissonance paradigm.

In one kind of cognitive dissonance experiment, two groups of subjects are asked to do something that they would not ordinarily do. One group is offered an explicit reward for doing it, while the other group is offered no reward, although subtle pressure is brought to make sure that virtually all the subjects agree to carry out the activity. An example is one of Totman's (1976a) experiments. He subjected student volunteers to a series of mildly painful stimulations of the skin. After several of these stimulations the subjects were told that part of the experiment included seeing if an injection of a new drug would relieve the pain. Half the subjects were paid for receiving the injection, while the other half were told that they could have it if they liked, but they need not, as their participation in the experiment would be just as useful as 'control' subjects, if they chose not to have the injection. Enough oblique pressure was put on the subjects so that almost all agreed to have the injection. In fact the injection was not a drug at all, but was a placebo, a substance with no physiological effect.

Totman found that those who had 'voluntarily' agreed to the injection both rated the stimulations less painful subjectively, and showed smaller physiological measures of pain stimulation (the galvanic skin response) than the subjects who had been paid. He argued that subjects who are paid have a ready-made explanation for why they accepted the injection. They were paid to do it. The other subjects are forced to attribute the decision to their own free will and therefore as part of the rationalization procedure they bring the rest of their experience into line as well. They are committed to the stimulations being less painful. Although this effect is not well understood, perhaps it occurs because for most of our lives, we choose our actions, anticipate their consequences, and are able to give reasons for both actions and consequences. So if we have decided to take a pain-relieving injection, our experience then becomes consistent with what we anticipate.

Totman (1976b) repeated this kind of experiment with hospital patients. Patients who had been having difficulty in sleeping were asked to volunteer for a trial of two different kinds of 'sleeping pill'. In fact they were offered two kinds of placebo pill with no physiological effects. After two nights on one of the pills, some of the patients were told they could decide to change to the other pill, which might be better, but they were told this would ruin the trial. But in the next three days they enjoyed an average of 1.3 hours more sleep than those who did not have to make a decision.

Again, therefore, the people in the group with no apparent external justification are left only to justify their actions in terms of their own, difficult choice, and these people show larger effects. Totman (1979) argues that many famous 'cures' of faith healers, pilgrimages and the like can be explained in this way.

Totman (1982) extended the argument to psychotherapy. As a result of social pressure, people find themselves doing things that they would not ordinarily do, but the therapist will have left them no alternative but to attribute the decisions to their own free choice. Therefore the person unconsciously makes all the other aspects of the experience consonant with the decision. So Totman would say that Cindy heard the sound of birds singing because *she* had decided to walk to the park the second time. She found herself feeling less frightened of what she imagined people were thinking about her because *she* decided to write down her thoughts. All the time the therapist has to keep up the pressure to ensure that she is likely to do these things, but to do so subtly so that Cindy experiences the decisions as her own.

Totman's argument that the client must make an attribution of any changes herself, and to her own choice, is fundamental to therapy. It is another way of speaking about the reowning of a sense of agency and experience that has been lost.

The second part of Totman's argument, however, is questionable. It neglects the fact that it is the client who undertakes therapy, enlists the therapist as an aid, a kind of auxiliary self who will share the responsibility of risky actions, a bit as a parent can do for a child.

If we were to accept Totman's complete analogy with cognitive dissonance experiments, we would have to accept that therapists were engaged, knowingly or otherwise, in a devious application of social pressure, which they concealed from the client.

Totman is wrong, however, in supposing that therapy requires that therapists covertly apply social pressure. Some may do, but this is not a necessary part of the procedure. There need be nothing going on behind the scenes, hidden from the client. But rather the therapist simply takes up the issues put to her by the client, supporting her endeavour, while not either giving in to symptoms or arousing resentments as bossy or controlling people are likely to do.

Cindy was outwardly meek, and felt incompetent in many activities. At the same time she felt defiant towards other people, who came to include the therapist. As therapy continued some of this crystallized out of the fog of panicky feelings of which she complained.

One might guess that her bids for autonomy and recognition in her family had been disconfirmed and disappointed, and had necessarily gone underground to emerge both as an overwhelming anxiety about what others were thinking about her, and as a determination not to give in. Her defiance indeed showed that she had not given up her desire for autonomy. It was the expression of a determined fighting back, and provided her with the powerful weapon of illness.

For therapy to be successful would be for her to discover her autonomy, to be able to assert herself in ways that did not involve her being ill, and for her to discover in others' relations with her a respect which she had felt hitherto absent from much of her life.

Non-directive therapy

Behavioural and cognitive therapy is easier to describe than psychoanalytic or existential therapy, because it appears to consist of procedures which the therapist suggests, and the client either does or does not comply with. Directive therapies differ principally in the kinds of things that therapists suggest. Behaviourists suggest actions, such as relaxation for tension, going out for agoraphobic people, returning things to shops for people who are afraid of asserting themselves (assertion training), and so on. Cognitive therapists tend to use the same kinds of idea, but supplement suggestions for action with suggestions for getting clients to talk to themselves in different ways, or for getting them to write down distressing thought patterns. Other directive therapists, such as Gestalt therapists, bioenergetic therapists or hypnotherapists, suggest other kinds of things, and Kovel (1976) or Herink (1980) give descriptions of these kinds of direct suggestion.

The second broad class of therapy is non-directive. It is sometimes called insight therapy. It is more difficult to describe since the therapist seems not to 'do' nearly so much. Instead she speaks back to the client about things that the client has already spoken of or implied.

Just as there is a range of directive therapies, there is a range of non-directive therapies. Perhaps the best known are Rogerian therapy; psychoanalytic therapy which itself has many schools, Freudian, Jungian, Kleinian, Lacanian; and existential/phenomenological therapy, influenced by Laing and a range of continental philosophers.

The starting-point of all these therapies is that the therapist does not suggest anything very much, but rather listens, and takes part with the client in exploring and experiencing what is going on between them.

Rogers's client-centred therapy (1951, 1961) is the easiest to describe. Therapy, in Rogers's formulation, takes place for a client who is anxiously in conflict or distressed, when three conditions occur in the therapy. They are that the therapist is genuine (and not defensive or professional), is accurately empathetic (able to enter into the client's framework and understand her feelings) and can give unconditional positive regard (is warm and accepting of the person, though not either approving or disapproving). When the client perceives these three characteristics, then therapy occurs. These three characteristics are, according to Rogers, both necessary and sufficient for therapy, not just of a Rogerian but of any other kind.

Why these are the conditions of therapy becomes clear in Rogers's view of the development of personality (see Oatley, 1981b). According to Rogers, people develop of their own accord. They have their own sources of growth and rightness. They will become who they can be, given only the right kind of conditions, rather as a tree becomes a tree of particular individuality, and recognizably of a particular species given appropriate conditions of soil and climate. What goes wrong for people is in the way that they are socialized. Parents know what is best for children, and will give or withhold love or approval according to whether the child does as they think best. So the child gives up acting according to his own desires and intuitions, and starts to construct a social self according to the demands placed on him. Conflict, or as Rogers calls it incongruence, between what a person actually is feeling but hides, and what she thinks she ought to do, causes the trouble. To hide something effectively one needs to hide it from oneself as well, so the person becomes alienated from herself. Incongruence is anxiety, self-doubt and despair.

So for Rogers, the therapist needs simply to avoid this coercive pressure on the person. Instead the therapist enters into the person's own world and accepts the client with warmth. To conduct therapy is to make this acceptance unconditional, and to do it genuinely. Under these conditions the client can grow. The plant does not need anyone pulling this branch out a bit longer, or trying to stuff that root more deeply into the soil.

In practice Rogerian therapists reflect back what clients say to them in slightly different words. Here for instance is a short exchange between Rogers and a male client, transcribed from a tape recording of their forty-eighth session together.

> CLIENT: I certainly have felt recently that I have more respect for, more objectivity toward my physical makeup. . . . It feels to me in the past I used to fight a certain tiredness I felt after supper. Well now I feel pretty sure that I really *am tired* – that I am not making myself tired – that I am just physiologically lower. It seemed I was just constantly criticising my tiredness.
>
> ROGERS: So you can let yourself *be* tired, instead of feeling along with it a kind of criticism of it.
>
> CLIENT: Yes, that I shouldn't be tired or something. And it seems in a way to be pretty profound that I can just not fight this tiredness and along with it goes a real feeling of *I've* got to slow down, too, so that being tired isn't such an awful thing.
> (Rogers, 1961, p. 116)

The therapist listens attentively, and takes part with the client in his self-exploration, which in turn reveals series of experiences and feelings that he had, as it were, lost touch with. As therapy proceeds the dialogue and the client's sense of himself become more fluid, and the client tends to start experiencing himself more independently, as more respecting of his own feelings, thoughts and emotions, and with enhanced self-esteem.

Psychoanalytic and existential/phenomenological therapies take the same non-directive stance of exploring meanings that emerge, though perhaps with more emphasis on the interpersonal meanings in the actual therapeutic relationship. Action is at the level of the verbal and non-verbal negotiations, which people do not always know about or refer to in relationships. Part of the aim therefore is to allow these negotiations to become explicitly spoken, to become conscious.

A brief fragment of a psychoanalytic therapy will point up further contrasts with the directive approach.

Psychoanalytic therapy

Mr Hal D went to a therapist at the age of 27 because he had been feeling that his life was futile. He felt stale at his work, and there seemed a danger that he would be sent by his company to an inferior job in another town.

59

After several months of therapy a number of things happened in his life. His father died, and very soon afterwards his mother started living with a man who had been a friend of the family. Hal was considerably upset by this. His mother and her new man were acting as if nothing unusual had happened, and expected him to do the same. Yet Hal felt there was something deeply inappropriate about his mother's liaison, and wondered if she had been having an affair before his father died. Shortly afterwards Hal had a violent argument with the woman at work with whom he was having a relationship, and they parted company.

Melancholy

Hal became more melancholy, saying that he found it difficult to see the point of going on living. The row with his woman friend had been over her being very influenced by her boss whom she also knew outside work. Her boss had said that Hal was emotionally unstable, drank too much, was unsuitable for her, and in any case was about to be posted to another town or perhaps even sacked, because he made trouble. Though Hal also felt that he wasn't very suitable for her, or probably for anyone else, he felt betrayed, and felt that it was better to be without anyone than to be with someone who was so easily influenced by others.

Hal's therapist felt puzzled, wondered in what way Hal was disappointed with her. But she could not put her finger on anything specific. He seemed so depressed, and she felt that it was best just to be there, and listen, occasionally making interpretations about how he felt let down and betrayed.

Towards the end of one session of long silences, in which almost all that he said was that he didn't really know what to say, he said he had had a dream, adding that he thought the therapist might like it.

He dreamed that he was asleep in the garden of the house where he had grown up. Though he was asleep he knew his mother came into the garden with some drinks. Mother somehow also turned into the friend with whom he had broken up. She had said, 'You can drink all you want in two hours' time', and then went off towards a long ditch that ran along one side of the garden.

The therapist asked Hal if anything came to mind about being asleep in the garden. He said he had sometimes slept in a deckchair in the garden in the summer, and also that he had watched *Hamlet* on the television the night before, so he supposed that he might have dreamed about the king being murdered in the garden while he was sleeping.

'Does anything else come to mind?'

'Not really.'

'What about the drinks?'

'I suppose I sometimes think I'll drink myself to death.'

'And that neither your mother, nor your woman friend, nor I would care very much.'

'Well I suppose you might feel a bit sorry, but not very much really.'

'What about the ditch in the dream?'

'There is a ditch along one side of our garden at home, that's all.' A slight note of petulance.

The therapist sat silently. Hal wondered what she was going to say. Finally she said, 'It sounds as if you're thinking of leaving. We've got two more sessions, two more hours till the Easter holiday, and after that you'll be off. You'll just ditch me.'

'How do you mean?' Hal is a bit shocked.

'Well I'm thinking that I'm also in the dream like your woman friend and your mother, only it is more difficult to know that the woman is also me. And as well as feeling miserable recently you've been feeling bitter, and let down by people, your mother, your friend. . . . Only feeling resentful is more difficult to talk about than feeling sad. I wonder what it is that I have done to let you down?'

'Well you just sit there and don't say very much. It's hard to know if you are even interested.'

'So to have your revenge I'll be ditched along with the others, and then you can just drink yourself to death, and then when it's too late perhaps we will feel sorry.'

The therapist said this quite softly.

'It's just a job for you. You ended nearly five minutes before the proper time last session.'

'It sounds pretty important whether I care or not.'

'Yes.'

Hal didn't leave. He'd been feeling that therapy was not helping at all, and seemed rather irrelevant. He realized in this episode that he had often felt like leaving in the face of feeling uncared about, and that she was right that he had been thinking of not coming any more after Easter. He also felt somehow more recognized by his therapist, or at least that she understood how he felt disappointed. She was neither dismissive nor 'professional', and in that moment he saw her somewhat differently from before.

In this kind of therapy the therapist pays attention to and speaks mainly of the relationship between them. Non-directive therapy of this kind, therefore, sets itself the task, not of influencing the client, but of speaking meaningfully in a dialogue, in which that person's truth emerges, even though hemmed about with lies, withholdingness, evasions and those peculiar devices which speak their own language, symptoms.

The only rule the therapist makes is that the client should come along and say whatever occurs to her, just as Freud asked his friend in the *aliquis* anecdote, described in the previous chapter.

Resistance and transference

The two terms that psychoanalytic therapists have for conceptualizing the relationship between them and their clients are 'resistance' and 'transference' (see for example Laplanche and Pontalis, 1973, Malan, 1979).

Resistance is usually defined as that which impedes the client in becoming conscious of things that she is unaware of, though the echo of the wartime use of the term is not fortuitous. Though the rule 'just come and say whatever comes to mind' seems simple and straightforward, indeed so simple that in some sense it is impossible to do anything else, the client finds she cannot. This inability is resistance.

Hal for instance by being silent in the session described above was being resistant, and it emerged that this was probably because he was feeling resentful that his therapist did not regard him as a person, but only as a 'patient' whom she saw in the course of her job. He felt particularly galled because he was so miserable, and felt strongly that this at least deserved a bit of sympathy. He did not feel like talking to her, though he experienced this as having nothing to say. He might also have avoided saying anything, or having anything come to mind, because he was frightened that if he criticized his therapist, she would retaliate in some way. And as most of us learn as children, the best thing in such circumstances is to lie low, to go along (apparently) with what is required of one, but to have absented oneself in some way.

By 'transference' analysts mean prototypical wishes and feelings, constructed in childhood, which replay themselves with a strong sense of immediacy in the relation with the therapist (Laplanche and Pontalis, 1973).

Resistance very often, as in the above fragment, takes on the form of transference.

Sulking

Thus if Hal's strategy in childhood was to withdraw inwardly when he felt disappointed, then this had provided a prototypical pattern of a symmetrical relating: 'You don't care – very well, I don't care either.' Symmetry and complementarity are, as Bateson (1935) has shown, two major axes of relating with another.

The ancient pattern of sulky withdrawal had also become a resistance in therapy. It is the withdrawal from the game which as Goffman (1961) pointed out, and which as described in chapter 2, takes the fun out of it for the other. But in this fragment, Hal is both unable to do anything different than sulk in this way, and he is unaware that he is doing it. But all sulking, all strikes, all passive resistance, are not much good unless the other is affected by them. Part of an analyst's practice is not simply to be drawn into roles offered by her clients in their interpersonal patterns, but instead to be aware of what is going on between them, to say so, and by speaking, show what the pattern may be.

In the face of this refusal of the therapist to be rattled by the sulk, Hal offers her a dream, a conciliatory gesture. It is well known that analysts like analysing dreams, though one might read a tone of faint sarcasm into his saying, 'I thought you might like it.'

And from the dream, in ways that Hal is not at first aware of, it emerges that this childhood strategy of sulking, of leaving the game, and even leaving in the most final and conclusive way possible, by suicide, are connected in a condensation, with his disappointment that the various women in his life, his mother, his woman friend and now his therapist have let him down.

What analysts call 'transference' is that wishes, thoughts, feelings, strategies are, as Freud (1905) said, 'new editions' of an old script (p. 158). While this script is in play, Hal acts towards an

63

imaginary figure described by object-relations theory, a figure who was inviting but is now disappointing. His withdrawal is the complement to this. It is not that Hal thinks the therapist is his mother, but he acts towards her as if she is. And her interpretation, if it is to make a difference to the truth between them, allows him to distinguish the therapist with whom he has agreed to come into therapy, from that more archaic image. This would be a resolution of transference, and the therapist's job is to aid that resolution by making interpretations of the aspects of their interpersonal relationship which seem founded on compulsive childhood patterns.

Thus Hal's therapist makes an interpretation when she says, 'So I'll be ditched along with the others.' This is both an interpretation in Freud's original sense of an interpretation of a dream, and it is an interpretation of the transference, which analytically oriented therapists regard as the major therapeutic procedure. It allows the client to become aware of what he is doing, particularly in his more intimate relationships, and at the same time to experience those relationships more fully.

Psychotherapy as an ethical activity

According to Haley (1963) and Totman (1982) psychotherapy is a sophisticated form of social influence. It needs to be sophisticated, because by putting forward the argument of symptoms, the client in psychotherapy has announced that she has taken her demands out of the realm of negotiation. So to help such people, therapists must practise yet more powerful manoeuvres to circumvent the resistance, to coax the client out of her illness, or to create conditions where the client will inadvertently find herself doing things she thought she could not do. In any case the therapist's job is to cause the client to change.

However, if both directive and non-directive therapies are ethical activities, clients are not some kind of sophisticated technical problem, as if the interpersonal were just some refractory version of the impersonal world, to be submitted to the human technical will, 'though for the clients' own good, of course'. The whole argument of therapy, and its difference from psychiatry (cf. Ingleby, 1981), is that symptoms are not treated as things or processes, which must be made to go away, but as a language to be understood. Just as Cindy's therapist, in effect, respected her defiance as assertion, and Hal's therapist recognized his suicidal despair as disappointment.

Though a person may choose to have a dentist treat her tooth as a thing, she does not want the expressions of her selfhood to be treated in the same way. It is usually disqualifications of that kind she was complaining of in the first place.

Suppose the issue were formulated not by asking how to get a client to change, but how to speak as one person who has her own will and individuality to another, but *without* the trappings of one person trying to get another to do something against her own will.

Suppose the question of therapy were formulated to ask how in a relationship might someone discover an experience of herself and the other, which she owned, rather than felt like disowning.

Therapy then becomes an ethical activity. First this means that therapy takes place in the world of *ethos*, and secondly it means that the activity itself is part of a search for right relations between people, for right action, but not just on the client's part, but on the part of both.

Ethos

Though the word 'psychotherapy' is modern, its roots in Greek are from '*psyche*' meaning 'livingness' and '*therapeia*' which meant 'healing' but which originally derived from the word for 'attendant' or 'companion'. So we could imagine that psychotherapy at root has to do with attending to someone's livingness. This attending is not an activity of finding out, or sorting out, or attempting to change anything going on in the client's mind. In terms of one of Aristotle's distinctions, the attending of therapy is an activity of practical science.

Aristotle distinguished between three kinds of knowledge or science. One category was of mathematics and the natural world, and is what we mostly think of now as natural science. Another he called 'productive knowledge' and corresponds to technology, where there are specific ends and techniques to reach them. But as Heaton (1979) has argued, psychotherapy has to do with neither of these, but with a third kind of knowledge that Aristotle called 'practical', which includes ethics and politics, and has to do with people's actions and interactions.

In the natural world which Aristotle called '*phusis*' from which comes the word 'physics', events are caused by external agencies which physicists nowadays call forces. The human world however is the world of *ethos* meaning custom, and here movement is from within the structures of the community, not like a movement in response to an externally imposed force.

In the domain of *ethos*, that is to say the ethical, we are concerned with customs or as social scientists now say, with rules, and with meanings. Whereas with physical mechanisms, the interest is in causes and explanations, in the domain of *ethos*, the concern is with meanings, because these are what people generate by acting intentionally within a mutually known and accepted set of rules. So for instance, if someone phones and leaves a message to ask the person to whom she wished to speak to phone back, the unspoken rule in our culture is that this should be done. Not to phone back is an action with a meaning: typically that the person who first phoned is not very important in the second person's life, although this might be difficult and embarrassing for them both to talk about, so that excuses become preferable.

Although we are partly physical and physiological, we are cultural too. And it is to the cultural sense of rules and meanings that the therapist speaks. The task of therapy is to establish first a rapport, a mutuality of accepted rules and customs for the activity of therapy, and secondly within that mutuality to discover the meanings that emerge. Within this formulation it is not that anything has gone wrong with the person and needs to be put right by applying some corrective cause or influence, as if the person were a thing. Rather, meaning needs to be discovered. Within this view symptoms are the symptoms of a person's meaning being lost or distorted by contradictions, disqualifications, excuses and the like in the community in which she has grown up. Though a person might feel that aspects of her life are just caused, and that they have no human intention or meaning, it is precisely the insight of both directive and non-directive therapy, that reclaiming intentions in what seemed simply to be caused by something outside us, liberates us from the sense of feeling them simply being done to us. It involves as Bateson (1971) suggested a wider view of the self than that of the skin-encapsulated, conscious ego.

Causes versus intentions

So psychotherapy is not a technical discipline. To conduct a technical activity one has to have a clear end in sight and then apply appropriate causal manipulations: as one might do when making a shelf capable of holding a certain weight of books perhaps. But in therapy as in parenthood it would be ridiculous and destructive to suppose that one could control what the product of one's ministrations was going to be like, or to have some technical plan of how to achieve that end. Though even non-directive therapists sometimes speak of 'technique', they mean really their approach to therapy; not the idea that they will cause the client change in closely defined ways.

It is possible to see what is wrong with attributing behaviour to causes in the following example of Edgley (1981). If I quite often go to the theatre with a particular friend, and she phones me up to see if I have got the tickets, I would not give an account of my theatre-going behaviour in terms of natural science. To do so might sound somewhat as follows: 'I observe that the purchase of two theatre tickets followed by a phone call from my friend tends to cause me to get on the train.' Rather I would attribute this action of getting on the train to my intention of going to meet my friend and going to the theatre. So in the human world it is not to causes or tendencies of the natural scientific kind that we attribute our behaviour. Rather it is to intentions that we attribute our actions. Intentions are not forces acting from outside us. They arise from within; though whether from within an individual or a community is an issue to be left open for the moment.

Mutuality and customs

Therapy as an ethical activity typically involves just two kinds of movement. First the establishment of mutuality, the shared bases for a community of at least two people. Second, the discovery of meanings within the customs or rules of this contained community.

For directive therapists the establishment of mutuality can occur in the meeting of a client wanting something to change in her life, and a therapist, perhaps a bit like a concerned parent who takes this seriously, and without any punitiveness. Within what-

67

ever mutuality that may be established, a directive therapist makes suggestions and supports the person's experimentation with new rules, new customs: 'Try doing it a little at a time, try writing down the disturbing thoughts.' To start with, the client may do this because the therapist shares the responsibility for risky actions. But if they change her experience, they become her own, and can become incorporated into the customs of her own life. In so far as the therapist either is controlling, or reminds her of coercive people in her past, then the client is likely to become resistant or defiant, as Ms Cindy S did. And she is quite right to do so: the issue is her own autonomy, and a mutuality of respect, not doing the will of another person.

So directive therapists question the rules by which people live, rules like: 'If I go out there is a good chance I will panic and lose control', which have come to have a habitual structure, so that the person needs to protect herself from their consequences.

Regulative and constitutive rules

Non-directive therapists work not so much at the level of these rules by which a person runs her life, but on the ways in which these rules fit together. In philosophy individual rules by which someone runs her life are called regulative. They regulate how one acts. Perhaps their prototypes are the authoritative voices of parents, or in the *Iliad* of gods. But the higher level rules by which these regulative rules fit together, the meta-rules, are called 'constitutive'. Heaton (1979) has argued that the distinction between directive and non-directive therapies corresponds to this distinction between regulative and constitutive rules.

So for non-directive therapies, like Rogerian and psychoanalytic therapy, if mutuality is established, the task is to allow reflection on the constitutive rules by which a person takes up her life in society. This is done by paying attention to the meanings that emerge between client and therapist. It is usually the case that though people are aware of their regulative rules, they can be quite unaware of the constitutive rules. As Ryle (1982) puts it, we can be aware of tactics but unaware of larger-scale strategies around which our lives are organized. No doubt it was this that led Freud to his metaphors of wishes being buried, and needing to be excavated archaeologically. But it is not so much that they are buried, but as Horney (1942) has said they pervade everything. Whereas it is clear to Cindy that she does not go out because her heart might start overacting, it may be less clear that this is part of a more pervasive pattern in which she has devoted herself to the principle that she should protect herself from harm, at almost any cost by finding convincing reasons why she cannot do things. Or it may be unclear to Mr Hal D that the guiding principle in his important relationships is to withdraw in the face of disappointment. This move may be appropriate on some occasions: what is wrong is that Hal can do nothing other than this. It is compulsive. Such compulsive strategies are as Freud pointed out defensive: they keep one safe.

Indirect communication

For a non-directive therapist it is not a matter of suggesting new rules, but of allowing reflection on the constitutive structure of the rules that already exist, of bringing these pervasive principles into view. This does however create a paradox. If the therapist does not suggest anything directly, then what is she doing?

Kierkegaard (1846) put it like this:

> To stop a man in the street and stand still while talking to him, is not so difficult as to say something to a passer-by in passing, without standing still, and without attempting to persuade him to go the same way, but giving him instead an impulse to go precisely his own way. (p. 247)

The assumption is that of two independent people, not one person taking control of the life or actions of another.

Such communications Kierkegaard called 'indirect', perhaps echoing Plato's notion discussed in chapter 1 of the impossibility of saying or writing down directly important issues of human relating and action. Indirect communication contrasts with the direct communications of advice, suggestion, persuasion and so on in which one person is trying to get the other to do something. One view of more radical non-directive therapists is that suggestions and pressure of any kind amount to trying to cause something to happen as a result of direct influence, and thus treating the person more like a thing in the world of physics than a person in the world of *ethos*.

To speak of an image coming to mind, or a feeling, to tell an allegory, or present a metaphor, to take part in play, or to speak ironically in a way that allows the other person to reflect, is what Kierkegaard meant by the indirect. These are proper forms of communication among people.

Learning and meta-learning

To put this in another way, behaviour and cognitive therapists talk about maladaptive and adaptive learning. Some people have become stuck in their lives, disengaged from the ordinary activities and customs of their community. So a therapist's role could be educational, and many behaviour and cognitive therapists see it in this way. Non-directive therapy, however, sees its role differently. Szasz (1965) calls it a meta-education: not the rules and actions themselves, but the ways in which they fit together are attended to. Thus connections and disconnections, contradictions, slips, errors, symptoms, all come to be the subject of attention, not the learning of new material. The meaning of these is that there are internal disharmonies among regulative rules. These rules are out of joint with one another, not properly articulated at the constitutive level, so the person is out of joint with herself and others. But one could not draw attention to this by suggesting further rules. Rather the client enters with the therapist into a reflection on such contradictions as they emerge in the relationship between them.

Neither learning nor meta-learning, however, can occur by applying causes to people. If we learn from our mistakes, then therapy had better be a situation in which mistakes can occur and be recognized, not be disapproved of, or punished. This in part is the importance of the containment, or mutuality of therapy. So therapy is the providing of this containment. From within it either spring new possibilities of action, or emerge new possibilities of interpersonal meaning.

Right action

'Ethical' also has a more common meaning: about doing the right or the good. And this too is germane to therapy. The same distinction between regulative and constitutive rules is useful. In some aspects of society we can organize our action by injunctions of various kinds; for instance by simple regulative rules like 'Drive on the left side of the road' or 'Do not steal'. There is a set of authoritative commandments such as these in our society, and a much larger number of more shifting informal rules of language and custom, by which we bring our world into being. But simply to know and follow the customs of a society is not to be alive. It neglects the fact that in some of our distress, in matters like envy, jealousy, pride or vengefulness, it would be pointless to try and stop these perturbations by just saying 'Don't do that'. It neglects also the issue of our engagement in what we are doing, the issue of authenticity.

The intuition of therapy, and particularly the non-directive therapies, is that it is by reflection rather than injunction that we come to terms with these matters. These therapies have to do with discovering not how to carry out particular procedures, but a coherence of rules at the constitutive level, a coherence which engages both the individual's desires, and the life of her community. Some kinds of incoherence, for example envy, jealousy and pride, are humanly inescapable. They disturb ourselves and our relations with others. They are not to be abolished. But they can be attended to, and in the attention possibilities of resolving a disrelation can occur.

While considering contradictions, it might not escape notice that there is something contradictory about what has been written in this chapter: the meeting of one person established as 'therapist' with another designated as 'client' might imply that the therapist has got it right. This is a stance behind which therapists may and sometimes do hide, perhaps seeming competent in a complementary role opposite to a client's feelings of incompetence. If a therapist does this, then the activity is flawed, becomes inauthentic, unethical. It is by attending to the mistaking of them both as they meet together that an equal dialogue is rediscovered. What analysts call transference may be a therapist's difficulties in understanding what the client is saying to her, a stagnation of the dialogue.

Buber's (1923) sense of the fundamental issue is that the interpersonal presencing of 'I' and 'thou' is to be regained. The world of reified symptoms, of things needing to be fixed, or even of the perspective from the third person 'she', useful for some purposes, can thereby lose the monopoly of influence.

Theories of therapeutic practice

Each therapist has a theory of principles of therapy, implicit or explicit, from which she works. The purpose of the theory is to give her a place to stand in her meeting with the client (cf. Oatley, 1981a). The theory might also aid the client by supplying concepts, terms and ideas that help in structuring her experience in ways which recover important meanings for her. But it is not part of the purpose of therapy to induct the client into the belief system of the therapist's theory. Induction into systems of belief is the role of parents, friends, teachers, elders in a community.

The purpose of a theory of therapeutic practice is to guide the therapist in her perceptions. A good theory is one that allows the client space for self-reflection and questioning in a dialogue which includes the manner of relating, and the possibility of each recognizing the other, but which does not become a battle, an argument or an indoctrination.

It remains to be discussed whether either directive or non-directive kinds of theory of therapeutic practice allow the accomplishment of what they set out to do, or whether these therapeutic practices are self-delusory screens behind which people who want to feel helpful may hide. One way of gaining a perspective on this is to listen to what clients say about therapy. Another, which often includes this source of information, is to take a perspective outside the therapeutic frame, an empirical perspective.

5

Outcome of therapy

'Does therapy work?' This question is asked by the hostile who suspect therapy is soft-minded indulgence, by the curious who might want to understand its intentions, by a potential client deciding whether to enter therapy, by a therapist who might want to know if what he is doing has effects.

Some non-directive therapists, particularly those of psycho-analytic or existentialist persuasions, might answer by saying that it is a misleading question – like asking whether friendship 'works', or the theatre 'works', or music 'works'. It is an activity that people take part in, which is important to them, which affects them, moves them, even transforms them. It doesn't make sense to ask if it works like asking whether some anti-corrosion treatment works in keeping rust off a car.

For other people, if therapy cannot be shown to be having effects that are beneficial in defined ways, then it is worthless. Therapists should either find something better to address these problems, or find something better to do as a job.

To ask whether therapy works may be confusing but it is not

stupid. It is more like the question 'Does education work?' In asking this one can be aware that all societies have had systems of education, formal or informal, ways of socializing people into the customs and knowledge of their particular cultural group. So in this sense asking if it works is senseless.

However, it does make sense to ask whether some particular form of education has the effect that is publicly claimed for it. Does the teaching of reading, writing and arithmetic 'work' in western society? Evidently 'yes' in the sense that a large proportion of the populations of those countries that attempt it are literate. But partly also 'no', in that large proportions of these populations claim 'not to be able to do maths'.

If therapy is a meta-education, it is quite appropriate to enquire what kinds of practice might enable this to take place: whether there are forms of practice which either impede or advance the meta-educational project. Does therapy better enable us to learn about our own learning in our personal relations?

So it is in this context that studies of outcomes of psychotherapy will be discussed.

Rogers's and Eysenck's influence on outcome research

Two sets of events have stimulated an explosion of research into the effects of psychotherapy. One was the work of Rogers (1951, 1961), starting in the late 1930s. Rogers formulated the principles of a non-directive therapy, as described in the previous chapter. He also started to become interested in empirical research into the effectiveness of therapy, and for instance introduced the idea of tape-recording sessions.

It has turned out to be possible for clients, or for independent assessors listening to tape recordings of therapy, to rate the extent to which therapists are or are not exhibiting the three Rogerian characteristics, of genuineness, warmth and empathy. It is also possible to measure whether clients' symptoms improve. So this formulation enabled some of the first research on the effectiveness of therapy to be carried out.

There is a large literature of research on Rogerian variables, see for instance Truax and Mitchell (1971); P.B. Smith (1981). In typical Rogerian experiments the outcomes for clients whose therapy sessions are rated as having high levels of the three

Rogerian factors are compared with those whose sessions had lower levels. Though there are problems of interpretation of this kind of result, namely that it may be that therapists feel more warm, straightforward and empathetic to patients who get better, the growing volume of research, as P.B. Smith (1981) indicates, shows that the Rogerian factors, though probably neither necessary nor sufficient, are important contributors to beneficial outcomes in therapy. Rogers has also been extremely influential in creating the climate for empirical research in psychotherapy.

Eysenck's challenge

A more controversial entrant into this arena was Eysenck. In 1952 he argued that there is a phenomenon of spontaneous remission, which is so marked that in a group of people suffering neurotic illness two-thirds of them will be better within two years without any therapy. He reviewed a selection of the published data on the outcomes of psychotherapy, mostly of the psychoanalytic kind. He concluded that on average two-thirds of therapy patients also improved in two years. So there really was no indication that therapy was doing anything beyond what would have happened without therapy. For an effect to be claimed, the rate of improvement under therapy must be better than the spontaneous remission rate.

Eysenck became interested in behaviour therapy, and by 1960 was arguing that this was the only kind of therapy that had any claim to rational consideration. It was scientific in that it was founded on principles of learning discovered experimentally in the laboratory.

Eysenck's papers not only catalysed research on psychotherapy outcomes, but also emphasized a dichotomy between behaviour therapy and insight therapy, which roughly corresponds to the distinction made in the last chapter between directive and non-directive therapy. The debate, and the research on which it depends, is now of considerable volume, making possible some evaluation of the field.

Bergin (1971) in a famous paper reviewed the same studies as Eysenck had, and showed how by choosing different criteria of 'improvement', one could either conclude, as Eysenck did, that therapy makes no difference, or that therapy is rather effective.

Evaluation is not easy. The questions as to what constitutes an adequate experimental design, and what might be appropriate measures of outcome are far from answered to everybody's satisfaction. Even reading the several hundred outcome studies is an enormous amount of work. Worse still they come to a range of somewhat different conclusions. By consciously or unconsciously choosing among them it has been possible for reviewers to come to different conclusions too, ranging from Eysenck's view that insight therapy does no real good, though behaviour therapy does, to the view that therapy is a procedure which has modestly positive effects, though specific therapies do not differ much in their effectiveness, to the view that most types of psychotherapy are effective, and different therapies have distinctively different effects.

The problem is not insuperable though. Many studies have been well constructed methodologically. In this chapter therefore, first a study that is generally considered the best outcome study of psychotherapy so far conducted will be described, that of Sloane *et al*. (1975). It is a study comparing a typical directive therapy (behaviour therapy) with a typical non-directive therapy (psychoanalytically oriented therapy). Then the meta-analysis of M.L. Smith, Glass and Miller (1980) will be assessed, as this does more than any other review to evaluate impartially most of the literature on therapeutic outcomes.

Sloane *et al*.'s outcome study

Sloane, Staples, Cristol, Yorkston and Whipple (1975) compared three groups of patients who had applied for therapy to an out-patient psychiatric clinic. The patients in the study were suffering from fairly severe disorders classifiable as neuroses or personality disorders of the kind thought to be amenable to psychotherapy. One hundred and twenty-six people were considered, but some were excluded as having disturbances which were too mild, or who were seeking therapy on mostly educational grounds. Others were excluded whose disturbances were not thought to be amenable to psychotherapy. People below the age of 18 or above the age of 45 were also excluded. In the end thirty patients matched for sex, and for high, intermediate and low degrees of psychopathology, together with four spare people in case of dropouts, were assigned to each of three groups.

One group was the Waiting List Group. These people were told that they would have to wait 4 months for treatment, but they had all the assessment interviews and were phoned every few weeks to ask how they were, and to say that they had not been forgotten. This group had many of the non-specific components of psycho-therapy – an expectation of improvement, assessment and contact with an interested friendly person.

The people in the second group, the directive, Behaviour Therapy Group, were given 4 months of once-weekly, hour-long sessions of behaviour therapy, including behavioural advice, re-laxation, desensitization and assertion training.

The third group was the non-directive, Insight Therapy Group. This therapy was a brief psychoanalytically oriented therapy of the same duration and frequency as the behaviour therapy. It avoided suggestions or advice, interpreted resistance, encouraged reports of dreams and did not undertake any direct retraining of any kind.

Therapy was carried out by three behaviour therapists and three psychoanalytically oriented therapists: experienced practi-tioners who had each treated a minimum of 250 patients and had at least 6 years' experience in the type of therapy which they were giving in this study.

The principal measures of psychological change were the Structured and Scaled Interview to Assess Maladjustment (SSIAM), which assessed disturbances in work and social rela-tionships, and a rating of the severity of target symptoms – specific symptoms which each patient complained about at the first assessment. Both the SSIAM and the target symptoms were rated by independent assessors, blind to which group the patient was in, at the beginning and end of therapy, and at a follow-up interview a year later. The patients themselves also completed a number of psychological scales. A close relative or friend was interviewed before and after the study, and the therapists also made assess-ments of the success or otherwise of their efforts.

Though the results of the study are complex in detail, their overall structure is clear. All three groups improved significantly in the severity of their target symptoms from their initial state. The two therapy groups improved significantly more than the Waiting

List Group. On the SSIAM scales the Behaviour Therapy Group was superior to the other groups though the difference was not significant. A year later the Behaviour Therapy Group was still significantly improved on target symptoms and the SSIAM ratings. The Insight Therapy Group were also improved on these measures, having continued to improve on the SSIAM rating which had not been much changed by the end of therapy. There are some problems of interpretation in the follow-up however, since by this time twenty-two of the Waiting List Group had chosen to have at least three sessions of therapy, and fifteen of the Behaviour Therapy Group and nine of the Insight Therapy Group had also had at least three extra sessions.

If anything the Behaviour Therapy Group had the slight edge of improvement over the Insight Therapy Group when compared with the control subjects in the Waiting List Group. However even in the Waiting List Group a fairly large amount of positive change took place, corresponding to a reduction in the mean severity of target symptoms from 'moderate' to 'mild'.

The kinds of target symptoms involved were problems of performance at work or college, sexual and social problems, fears of certain kinds of feeling or expression, for example anger, bodily complaints, anxieties and depressions.

In this study, a relatively brief therapy over 4 months was able to make a substantial change in people's lives. Although not everybody improved, the following are typical of those who did improve.

Tom Morton . . . liked his [behaviour] therapist's philosophy of life and this helped to crystallize his own. His loneliness, lack of values, and need to impress people as tops had all just about disappeared. He had moved away from home. There remained imperfections in his sexual life, but these struck the assessor as being less Tom's problem than his girl-friend's. He was much improved overall, but his mother told the research assistant that he had not changed and was very hyperactive. (pp. 113–14)

After four months [of insight therapy] Mary Teresa Moore had completely lost her obsessive thoughts about harming her children or herself. Her depression and anxiety were nearly gone, and in general she was almost completely recovered. She still felt a little guilt about sex but expected this to stop when she got married in three months, and she had a fine relationship with her fiancé. In summary, her rather severe symptoms had dramatically improved. (p. 115)

Whatever else one might want to say about all this, three things stand out. First, some aspects of therapy outcome can be assessed. Even though more subtle aspects of people's feelings are not captured in psychological measurements, or inter-group statistical comparisons, it was possible to conduct a research study which clearly took clients' own feelings and experiences into account. Though both clients' assessments and those of the therapists were somewhat more enthusiastic than those of the independent assessors, on most measures it was concluded that therapy had substantial benefits.

Secondly, however, even being on a waiting list for therapy had a moderate positive effect. Though in this experiment no comparison was made with no-contact controls, it seems that to make a decision to seek therapy, to have several detailed and sympathetic assessment interviews, and to have phone contact with a friendly and concerned person was responsible for a moderate improvement, perhaps rather like the one Eysenck claimed for spontaneous remission.

Thirdly, in this experiment no basis was found at all for the polemical argument made by behaviour therapists that insight therapy is worthless. When employed on similar populations of suitable patients who had themselves applied for therapy, equal involvements of the time of experienced therapists was accompanied by about the same degree of psychological change with either behavioural or psychoanalytically based therapy.

Though Sloane *et al.*'s study of outcome is one of the best that has been carried out, it has itself been criticized. Rachman and Wilson (1980), who favour a directive behavioural approach, argue that in terms of the measurements made, it adheres too closely to a 'disease' model and uses psychiatrically trained raters, whereas for a proper assessment measurements should be employed following Lang's (1970) psychological approach, rather than a medical one.

Lang proposed that fear and anxiety involve three different systems: the behavioural, the verbal and the physiological. Thus assessment should involve separate measures of the actual behaviour under question, verbal self-report scales, and physiological indices.

Perhaps the best sources, apart from these mentioned, for reading about the various approaches to empirical work on psychotherapy are the two *Handbooks of Psychotherapy and Behaviour Change*, by Bergin and Garfield (1971) and Garfield and Bergin (1978).

A quite different approach of the kind favoured by some non-directive therapists, particularly some in the psychoanalytic and existential-phenomenological traditions, is that empirical research, by trying to capture results in measurements and statistics, misses the human point of therapy altogether. The unravelling of interpersonal meanings which are the major issue of therapy is altogether neglected. For the reader of a book on psychotherapy as a human relationship, this point may have some force, and it is clear that the unfolding of meaning takes place not in group statistical comparisons, but in the stories of individuals and human interaction.

Some of the best portrayals of therapy of this kind have been books designed to be read as literature. First of course are Freud's famous case histories which established therapy as an unfolding story, for example the case of Dora (1905) or the Wolf-man (written up with additional material edited by Gardiner, 1972). In addition the following give vivid accounts of journeys within therapeutic relationships. *Dibs: In Search of Self* was written by the therapist Virginia Axline (1971). *I Never Promised You a Rose Garden* was written as a novel by Hannah Green (1964) who was the client in therapy. *Sybil* is a documentary account, by a third person, Flora Schreiber (1973) who knew both therapist and client. *Anna* is a more tragic story of a woman who finally committed suicide while attempting therapy, written by her husband, David Reed (1976). There seems a place for both empirical studies and personal accounts.

Even with the empirical approach, however, so difficult is it in the ordinary world to conduct clinical studies conforming to the canons both of humane therapy and experimental tidiness, and so impossible is it for any reviewer to read the literature without biases of one sort or the other, that a fresh way of assessing the hundreds of empirical outcome studies is needed. Such an approach, called meta-analysis, has now been undertaken by M.L. Smith *et al.* (1980).

Smith, Glass and Miller's meta-analysis

Smith *et al.* have taken the reviewing of studies of the effectiveness of psychotherapy into a new phase. Before their work reviewers had come to quite different conclusions as to the net results of outcome studies they had reviewed.

So, for instance, one well-known review by Rachman (1971) concluded that behavioural therapy was superior to other kinds. But double standards were used, requiring that non-behavioural treatments be compared with spontaneous remission rates, while no such criterion was applied to behavioural studies. Another review by Luborsky *et al.* (1975) counted the number of well-controlled studies which found for and against the effectiveness of therapy. They concluded that all the psychotherapies they reviewed benefited the clients. Other reviewers, like Bergin (1971), argued that the question 'Is therapy effective?' cannot be answered; only questions phrased in terms of whether some particular therapy, given by particular therapists, to some particular homogeneous group of clients stand any hope of being answered.

M.L. Smith *et al.* point out that before the idea of the controlled experiment, it had been similarly difficult sometimes to tell whether an investigator was just seeing what he wanted to see in the observations he made in a single study. But gradually the experiment, including carefully impartial sampling procedures and controls, came to be seen as a privileged generator of reliable information fit to be passed on from one person to another.

How odd it is therefore, that when addressing not the data of a single original investigation, but the data of many published studies, quite different standards should apply. Smith *et al.* therefore made the appropriate step, sampled impartially across the range of outcome studies and used statistical analyses to provide indices of net effects.

They set out at first to try and include all controlled outcome studies up to 1977. They fell short of this aim, but none the less achieved a representative sample. The main measure which they took was called the 'effect size'. It consisted of calculating the difference in the means between treated and control groups on each outcome measure used in each study, in terms of the standard deviation of the control group. Thus if, on some particular measure, the mean of a treatment group were exactly one standard deviation superior to the mean of the control group, this would be an effect size of plus one. It would mean that at the end of therapy, the average client who undertook therapy would be better off than 84 per cent of the people in the control group in terms of that measure.

Part of the value of this approach is that it defines a strict criterion for admission into the meta-analysis – namely that there must be at least two groups being compared. One group was given some described form of therapy, while the other drawn from the same population was either given no therapy, was put on a waiting list, or was given some alternative form of therapy. Psychotherapy was defined broadly as involving clients identified by themselves or others as having some emotional or behavioural problem, which was treated psychologically or behaviourally by someone identified as a therapist by virtue of training or affiliation. They found 475 studies meeting these criteria, which they estimated to be 75 per cent of the published literature.

Their main result was that of the 475 controlled studies, in which 1766 outcome measures were reported, the average effect size was 0.85 standard deviation units (p. 87). This means that the average client receiving therapy in these studies was better off than 80 per cent of the members of control groups on the measures studied. As Smith *et al*. point out, rather than supposing that the effects of therapy are rather modest, this is a large effect by ordinary standards of social science measurement. They quote estimates of the effects of 9 months' instruction on increasing reading achievement in elementary school as 0.67 standard deviation units and the effect of television on anti-social behaviour as 0.34 standard deviation units (p. 88).

Perhaps most interestingly, Smith *et al*. supply information from their meta-analysis of the effects of different kinds of therapy. Eclectic behaviour therapy (including assertiveness training) with 37 effect sizes found in the sample, produced a mean effect size of 0.84 standard deviations, and systematic desensitization with 373 effects being measured scored 1.05 standard deviation units. Standard psychoanalytic therapies with 108 effects measured produced a change of 0.69 standard deviation units. What Smith *et al*. called 'dynamic eclectic therapies', which used psychoanalytic and more relational ideas such as those described in this book, for example in the case of Mr Hal D, and which in the USA are influenced by Sullivan (1953), with 103 effects being measured produced a change of 0.89 standard deviation units (p. 89).

Neither behavioural nor psychoanalytically based therapies did best in this overall assessment of average effect sizes. The therapies producing the largest effects were cognitive therapies (see for example Ryle, 1982), and cognitive-behavioural therapies, such as those described for Ms Cindy S, with a mean effect size of 1.13 standard deviation units (p. 89).

Different therapies evidently had different kinds of effect. So for instance (p. 92) it was psychodynamic therapies which were found to do best of the various kinds tried with psychotic people. Cognitive therapies did best with people with a single simple phobia.

Looking at the kinds of changes produced (p. 93), Rogers's (1951) client-centred therapy did best on measures of self-esteem, cognitive therapies did best on measures of fear and anxiety, dynamic eclectic therapies did best for measures of work/school adjustment.

None of these is perhaps surprising for people who have sympathy for a range of therapies, since these areas tend to be the specific targets of each of the particular therapies involved. However the results indicate serious rethinking for therapists, if their therapy were not having any effect on the areas in which they were interested. They are also important for clients contemplating therapy of a particular kind.

Outcome studies in general indicate, as Shapiro (1980) says, effects of both specific factors due to the particular kinds of therapy, and some non-specific factors. The non-specific factors are large, and it is plausible to suppose that the most important of them is the relationship with the therapist.

One argument in the literature is that almost anything that a therapist does will have some beneficial effect on the client. It need not be a specific treatment at all. This non-specific effect is sometimes called a placebo, since it is similar to the inactive substances used in drug trails, as described in the previous chapter. When placebo treatments in the meta-analysis were compared with no treatment, they did moderately well – an effect size of 0.56 of a standard deviation (p. 89). People do improve without any specific treatment – though of course this does not mean that nothing is happening to them. Placebo effects also occur in drug therapies and provide a reason why all trials of psychoactive drugs are conducted against a control group with an inactive (placebo) drug.

The placebo effect includes a relationship with a therapist and the expectations of improvement. One way of grasping an overall sense of the outcome studies is that the more structured and extended relationships provided by specific therapies account for additional effects over and above the placebo effect.

Smith *et al.* were also able to see what features of outcome studies correlated with good outcomes, and might therefore be confounding factors, perhaps partly responsible for measured changes. Among potential confounding factors studied were age and intelligence of the clients, severity of the diagnosis, experience of the therapist, whether treatment was given individually or in groups, and a dimension called 'reactivity' which was the degree to which the measurement used might itself be subject to suggestion. Considering the amount of heat generated in discussion of such factors as these, most of them were found to contribute somewhat little to the outcome. The most serious contaminant was the reactivity of the measure used. More suggestible, softer measures were associated with better outcomes.

With this issue in mind Smith *et al.* could consider the relatively small group of studies which included Sloane *et al.*'s in which a behavioural and an insight therapy were directly compared on the same population of clients. On average the behavioural therapies did better than insight ones when compared directly. However, this superiority was evident only on the more suggestible measures. When compared using only the less suggestible measures the advantage of the behavioural over the verbal therapies fell to 0.04 of a standard deviation (p. 107).

Finally Smith *et al.* reviewed studies in which drugs were compared with a placebo, drugs were compared with psychotherapy, or drugs and psychotherapy combined were compared with a placebo. Again they produced a rather surprising finding that even in such studies, where patients tend to be hospitalized and correspondingly with more severe diagnoses than many of the clients in the psychotherapy meta-analysis, psychotherapy does quite well. They estimated that the average effect of psychoactive drugs (anti-psychotic, anti-anxiety and anti-depressant) over and above a placebo effect is 0.44 of a standard deviation. The effect of psychotherapy in these studies was 0.32 of a standard deviation above the placebo effect; the effect of drugs and psychotherapy combined was 0.62 above the placebo effect – almost as large as the sum of the two effects acting independently (p. 170).

The role of empirical studies of therapy

It would be a mistake to suppose that experimental studies of the outcomes of therapy are the only reliable guide to understanding. It would be a mistake for two reasons. First, in the human world there are many sources of knowledge and understanding, more direct, more informative, more intimate than those gained in any experiment. In the natural world the experiment is used to probe nature, to investigate it, to arrange conditions so that amid the flux of tendencies and causes some particular causes will be actualized and come into measurable view (cf. Bhaskar, 1975). People could scarcely have understood the properties of chemical combination, the propagation of the nerve impulse or a thousand other matters were it not for experiment.

In the natural world scientists have introduced the idea of natural law – it is not a law that can be obeyed or disobeyed. It is a generalized, descriptive statement of regularity, with a view to explanation in terms of causes and tendencies, irrespective of certain contexts such as who is making the relevant observations.

In the human world the same word 'law' occurs, but it has a quite different character. It is not descriptive, it is a publicly recognized regulative rule. It describes what should happen in a particular culture, and it is to be obeyed or disobeyed. So it becomes inappropriate to do experiments in order to discover social laws or rules. If one wants to know what the social laws are in any society one may ask, or observe or interpret – it is a matter of discovering meaning, not mechanism, although when aggregations of people are studied as in therapy outcome studies, effects sometimes act with regularities that can be described, rather loosely, as being due to causes and tendencies.

The function of experiments like that of Sloane *et al.*, as Smith *et al.* argue, is not to provide the basis of causal explanations, but to provide evaluations in a critical discussion of therapists' generalizations. Examples of such generalizations are easy to find. 'Psychoanalysis is an expensive waste of time, it is no better than spontaneous remission.' 'Transference interpretations are the only interventions that have truly mutative effects.' 'Behaviour therapy is clearly superior to other kinds and furthermore it demonstrates its effects in objective measures of outcome.' 'It is counter productive to attempt psychotherapy if the patient is on drugs.' 'Psychotherapy is harmful for psychotic patients.' These sentiments and many more, uttered with great assurance as generalizations, are meant to go beyond the individuality of any particular encounter of therapist with client and to describe an aspect of human universals at the level of people's abilities to change.

Experiments on the outcome of therapy imply that the statements quoted in the previous paragraph are ungrounded in evidence. Instead other evaluations were given evidential grounding. With the exceptions of some forms of therapy which were associated with no particular theory, and were classified as 'undifferentiated' most established therapies produce effects larger than a placebo effect. They do benefit clients in a number of ways, some of which can be measured.

Though natural scientists are willing to subject generalizations to empirical test in order to refute them, therapists seem less willing to do so. Therapy provides a safe and laboratory-like setting in which a client may test his interpersonal theories against the actuality of a therapist, who will not necessarily fit in with them. In so doing his theories are enabled to change (Oatley, 1982). Consciousness may be increased.

The evaluative studies of therapy allow therapists to subject their theories of therapeutic practice to public critical discussion. One function of these studies, therefore, is to raise the consciousness of therapists. Those who complacently think they have the monopoly of beneficial practice might reconsider.

A second issue from these experiments is that by casting the practice of psychotherapy into an experimental framework, they may tempt a therapist to suppose that therapy is a technical matter: that he might decide on the basis of an experimental result to do some specific kind of thing in order to influence the behaviour of his client more closely and more predictably, as suggested by Shapiro (1980). This argument is a difficult one though. For instance a therapist working with a client whose self-esteem was at a low ebb, and finding that Rogers's form of client-centred therapy is effective in raising people's self-esteem, might decide that he should increase the level of the three Rogerian variables in his behaviour, become warmer, give more unconditional positive regard and be more genuine. Yet how could one decide just to do any of these things? One either is or is not genuine or phoney. To decide to act more genuinely has an indelible streak of the phoney about it. People are not things to whom technical solutions are to be applied.

Though therapies with quite different modes of practice, and quite different theoretical bases can produce effects which are similar in size and in types of measurable benefit, this does not mean that it makes no difference how therapy is practised. It makes a profound difference both to the therapist who finds in a particular therapeutic theory a ground on which to meet his client and articulate the meanings that emerge, and to the client. Evaluation studies are not an argument for uncritical eclecticism. They are an argument for self-criticism, mutual respect and an openness of discussion among therapists, which has begun to take place, and which has removed some of the mystification of therapy.

Smith *et al.* say that therapy

> may not educate as well as schools; it may not produce goods and services as well as management science; it may not cure illnesses as well as medicine; but it reaches a part of life that nothing else touches as well. (p. 184)

In the life in between self and other, it is the client's own stirrings towards change and wholeness that are touched, not anything being done to him by a therapist. So one can conclude from these empirical studies that these stirrings of autonomy and responsibility can be met and engaged with, in a number of different ways. The therapist discovers in these studies that he takes part, the humbler part in the relationship. He hopes to make a difference, but he is not a cause of change.

6

The life of groups

Though group therapy takes place, like individual therapy, when people who find themselves in emotional difficulties consult a therapist, groups have also expanded in a quite different way. In the 1960s and early 1970s they seemed in some parts of the USA and Europe to have become harbingers of a new social order. Carl Rogers in 1968 proposed that the 'intensive group experience [is] perhaps the most significant social invention of this century' (p. 268).

Not only people feeling stuck in their lives or people in emotional crises, but also people who would never consider individual therapy started going to groups for purposes of 'personal growth'. Groups became, as one phrase had it, 'therapy for normals'.

'Growth centres' sprang up, sponsoring a range of group activities, named T-groups, encounter groups, sensitivity groups or awareness groups. Though the names differ, they stand for similar kinds of intensive experience, in which people meet to change, to become as they say 'more in touch with their feelings', to embrace values of interpersonal directness and honesty. Perhaps as an antidote to aspects of adult life, they seek to recreate something of the warmth, excitement, intensity and engagement of childlike play.

Group methods were introduced into organizations, for the training of interpersonal skills among colleagues, or between management and employees, or between company people and customers. They were introduced into schools as an adjunct or even in some cases as a replacement of more traditional methods of education (see for example Rogers, 1951, 1961), into colleges and universities, as an adjunct to the academic syllabus, and into the training of social workers and professional psychologists.

In this book all these developments will be treated as branches of the same therapeutic tree. Although they do not all address clinical populations, their aims and methods are similar: the aims are to encourage personal and interpersonal transformation, not just learning about specific material. Their methods are to provide environments in which the personal and the interpersonal are specifically attended to.

The experience of a group

What is it like to go to an encounter or sensitivity group? The first time one goes, it might seem quite strange. So one might imagine a person who has not been to a group before: Ms Emma H. She went to a group on the recommendation of a friend, Eileen.

Emma felt that she lacked confidence in social situations, and often got depressed for no apparent reason, though she felt rather obscurely that this had something to do with her relationship with her husband Tom.

Her friend Eileen had enthused about groups. She said they had helped her feel a lot better about herself. Emma did not much like a strain of 'groupy' talk which her friend tended to lapse into, going on about 'getting into her feelings', 'working through her stuff' and the like. At the same time she sensed that something important and enlivening had taken place for Eileen. Besides, she made it clear that the groups she had been to were exciting and fun, and Emma felt her life becoming humdrum.

So she decided to make a reservation and go. When she arrived, she entered a carpeted room, with a circle of cushions on the floor.

Already sitting on some of them were several people, waiting. They did not say much, though one said 'Hello' and a couple of others acknowledged her arrival by smiling. She noticed that three people had taken their shoes off. Other people arrived, and some of the new arrivals also took their shoes off, then selected a cushion and sat on it. Emma wondered if she should have removed her shoes, looked round and was reassured to see that others too still had their shoes on. The mood of somewhat apprehensive waiting continued. Emma felt very anxious, and wondered about leaving, before she was committed.

She whispered instead to the woman who had said 'Hello' when she arrived, 'When does the group start?'

'Oh, it starts when you get in', she said, and smiled.

A little later the same woman announced, 'I'm going to be leading the group this weekend. My name is Christine. I don't know exactly what's going to happen here, except that we will probably get to know each other, and perhaps ourselves and how we relate to others quite a bit better. I'm feeling a bit tense at the moment, and I'm also looking forward to being with you. I think that's all I want to say just now.'

Emma was puzzled by this. A long silence followed. At last somebody said to Christine, 'Wouldn't it be a good idea to introduce ourselves?' She replied, 'Are you saying you'd like to introduce yourself?' The speaker said, 'Oh all right then, if it has to be me first', as if the leader had asked him to introduce himself. He told the group his name was Ian Edwards and that he was a teacher at a comprehensive school. Other people round the circle introduced themselves in the same kind of way, until someone said, 'I don't really want to say my occupation, I feel that just stereotypes me. I'll just say my name: Thea.'

The other people in the group including Emma said something about themselves, then there was another long silence.

More than an hour was taken up with people discussing what they might all do in the group. The discussion was sporadic, and interspersed with rather tense silences. Occasionally people asked the leader what they should do. One man who had been to a group before suggested that the group should play what he called a 'warm-up game'. But nobody took his suggestion up, though there was some discussion about what kind of game he might have in mind.

After the group had been going for about two hours and Emma was wondering whether they would be able to stop and have some coffee soon, Ian, the man who had said he was a comprehensive school teacher said to the leader quite angrily, 'You say you're the leader but you've hardly done anything since you've been here. You know what goes on at these groups, but you won't tell us.'

Christine said in an even tone, 'Well, I understand that people feel rather frustrated with me, and that this fencing and manoeuvring we are doing is uncomfortable. I suppose I could have prevented it by coming with an agenda, and told everybody, "Now we'll do this or discuss that", but as a leader I'm in an influential position, and to do that might quite effectively have prevented anybody else from doing or saying what they wanted, and though you're right that this situation isn't unfamiliar to me, I don't think I could have any idea why each of you came to the group, or what each of you wanted to do here.'

At this point the atmosphere changed perceptibly. One of the members, Alan, who said he was a student, started to talk about how confused he felt at college, and how inadequate he felt when there were a lot of people in a seminar or meeting, although there were parts of his course he liked. He had come to the group to see if he could practise talking in a group of people, so that perhaps he did not feel so threatened. Various people sympathetically started asking him about college, and he started talking about his life there. Emma stopped wondering if she would slip off home when coffee time came. She found herself listening more closely to Alan speaking about things that were important to him.

The structure of groups

Groups are different, but many of them start somewhat like this, and go through an evolution from defensiveness, to people talking to one another about their concerns, to the participants engaging with each other in what is going on between them. Mysteriously, as often as not, rather than staying as a collection of individuals meeting together, the group takes on a life of its own, in which what goes on both for the people there and among them becomes intensely fascinating, often to the surprise of people who thought that without an agenda there would not be anything to do. A group is occasionally frustrating or boring, occasionally very moving, occasionally hilarious. Often by the end the members feel they do indeed know themselves better, usually feel more open, and delighted to have known some other people in ways not easily attained in ordinary conversations.

How might we conceive participation in a therapeutic or growth group? It might be that in such groups clients each have one-to-one relationships with the group leader, and that when working with the leader they do so in front of an audience consisting of the other members of the group. Alternatively by working with a group the leader may address several people at the same time perhaps offering suggestions if she is a directive therapist, or making interpretations about the group's relationship to her if she is a psychoanalyst. Such activities are really modifications of individual work for the purposes of groups, and they do indeed occur very frequently. The goals and outcomes of one-to-one therapy, of work with individuals in groups, and of more group interactive methods, are in many ways rather similar. However, in this and the next two chapters mainly the aspects of groups that are intrinsic to group interaction will be discussed, not the practices which are primarily modifications of individual therapy. It is this that guides the choice of sensitivity and encounter groups for the second half of this book, since the experience of these groups differs markedly from individual therapy.

A group will be defined here as a number of people meeting together, either with or without a designated leader, for purposes which include attending to their own interpersonal behaviour, thoughts and feelings within the group.

Characteristically groups of this kind contain between six and twenty people who sit in a circle. They may meet together continuously with breaks for meals and sleep over a whole weekend, or a week in some residential setting, or the group may meet weekly for one to three hours, perhaps for most of a year.

Members of groups meeting together for various purposes and paying attention to what they are thinking and feeling, and what is going on between them have occurred for thousands of years. They may indeed be as old as the human species. If humanity necessarily involves the creation of cultural rules, along with their discussion and modification, then participatory group activity is as fundamental to being human as language, to which such activities are intimately related. Certainly most known cultures generate social gatherings of various kinds for the purposes of religion, or ceremonial, or festival. The main difference of these kinds of meetings from the groups discussed here is that in most human gatherings participants typically refer to some purpose other than reflective participation. By contrast, in the groups discussed here it is the reflective participation itself which is the purpose of the meeting.

Origins of group practice

Though groups of this kind include many elements of cultural groups throughout the ages, it is generally thought that meeting principally for the purpose of self-reflection is quite modern. Histories of groups tend to refer to various founders, most frequently Joseph Pratt, Jacob Moreno and Kurt Lewin (see for example Shaffer and Galinsky, 1974).

Pratt was a doctor who in 1905 began organizing poor tuberculosis patients into groups, at first for the purposes of instructing them on principles of diet, exercise and the like. But in the course of his work he came gradually to realize the importance of the resources of the group itself – the atmosphere of mutual support, the sharing of experience and the beneficial effect that the improvement of one group member had on the others. It is perhaps the influence of Pratt's work which made group therapy such a commonplace of hospital psychiatric treatment.

Even more important in terms of his wide influence, and his prodigious invention of many of the ideas, concepts and methods which are now as fundamental in groups as Freud's ideas on therapeutic technique have been in individual therapy, was Moreno. One of his characteristic inventions is psychodrama (see Greenberg, 1974), a theatrical form in which a protagonist acts out conflicts or problems in her life, with other participants taking on supporting roles in unscripted dramatic situations that unfold. He introduced the technique of role-playing which by now has become an important part of many kinds of training and therapeutic activities. He also coined the terms 'encounter' and 'group therapy'.

Groups started as a movement within social psychology in a way that was soon to spill over into therapy and more popular culture at the end of the last war, in the USA under the influence of Lewin.

93

The story of the first group of this kind which became known as a T-group, where 'T' stands for 'training' or 'sensitivity training', is told by Benne (1964). Lewin with several colleagues familiar with Moreno's techniques were conducting a workshop on problems arising from the recently enacted Fair Employment Practices Act, in which participants role-played various situations that might arise. In the evenings Lewin and his colleagues met to discuss their perceptions of the day's events. Some of the participants asked if they could join in the evening discussions. These sessions now included perceptions from all participants not just the professional leaders, and it was generally felt that they were the best part of the workshop.

Out of these elements were born encounter groups such as those associated with Schutz (1971) and the California growth centre at Esalen. Many other offshoots cross-pollinated with psychoanalytic and phenomenological ideas to form the many humanistic therapies, self-help organizations and growth centres which exist today.

The Theatre of Spontaneity

Perhaps the attribute which most readily distinguishes group participation from individual therapy, an attribute which has characterized the encounter group movement, is playful spontaneity: the living 'in the here and now' as Moreno's phrase has it. Groups in practice are very often playful and emotionally warm. No doubt this contributed to their popularity.

This is not a difference in intent: Freud's idea of free association is precisely an injunction to spontaneity, and for many subsequent theorists too, notably Bateson (1955) and Winnicott (1971) the essence of therapy is play. In groups the activity of being able to play together is more easily attained than in some forms of one-to-one therapy.

Moreno grew up in Vienna at the time when Freud was at the summit of his career: he started to develop his ideas as a premedical student, taking part in fantasy play with children in public parks. In 1921 he opened his 'Theatre of Spontaneity' as a new art form (see for example Moreno, 1940). He came to regard the conventional theatre as stultifying and uncreative, with its prepared scripts and rehearsals. After one of his actress's personal problems was brought to his attention, he conceived the idea of unscripted role-playing as a means for working through such problems. So psychodrama as therapy was born.

As psychodrama developed, Moreno came to see psychoanalysis too as stultifying – placing the client in a passive position, encouraging rumination and triviality – whereas in action, people could become aware of unsuspected aspects of themselves. This principle of awareness through dramatization has been one which has tended to separate the humanistic therapies from psychoanalytically oriented therapies.

The idea of dramatizing that which is problematic is complementary to Freud's theory of interpretation. In a psychoanalytic interpretation, as in the fragment of Mr Hal D's therapy in chapter 4, Hal's therapist became aware that he was thinking of leaving therapy, as if to take revenge. The therapist says, 'To have your revenge I'll be ditched along with the others'. As Strachey (1934) has pointed out, to be therapeutic the therapist's interpretation would enable the client to experience the difference between the present figure of the therapist and the fantasy through which he was seeing her. Simultaneously, in that moment the client is aware of the two modes of being with his therapist: a mode of two adults in a room and another mode enacting an embitterment born of childhood disappointment.

In dramatization unsuspected aspects of people's habitual modes of relating come into play, but by a different means of the person herself enacting, and perhaps exaggerating, the conflictual or the problematic. An awareness grows that the action that takes place both is and is not fantasy; both is and is not real. As such it can move beyond the stuck, the anxious and the inescapable.

Group games

Quite often groups play games which are organized almost like children's party games. Some leaders have a repertoire of games which they invoke during the group, and indeed there are books which are compendia of group games (for example Lewis and Streitfield, 1970).

Some popular games have to do with trust and distrust, with inclusion and exclusion, and with dramatizations of conflict.

Perhaps the best-known group game is one in which the group stands in a circle while individual members take it in turns to stand with their eyes shut, and without moving their feet to fall passively towards the circle of the group. A person falling in this way has the rather delicious sense both of being able to let go, and when she reaches an angle at which she would certainly fall if she did not move her feet, of being caught and supported by some unknown other. The person catching her then pushes her back towards and beyond the centre of the circle to be caught by someone else. The person in the middle sways back and forth like an inverted pendulum between the members of the circle.

The game is thought to have to do with trust: a person too untrusting to let herself go will find herself refusing to play in the middle, or if she does, she may find she moves her feet before she has fallen very far. For this game to be played, the person in the middle does have to trust. And the people in the circle do have to be, in the terms of the game, trustworthy. If someone is not paying attention, the person in the middle can be dropped and fall.

Within the rules of the game a small drama of the possibility of letting oneself go, and falling towards the other can be played out – perhaps a metaphor, enacted and not just spoken about, for other acts of letting oneself go that one either allows or does not allow.

Another game is about interruption. People sit in threes, and the instructions are that one of the trio talks about something (anything she chooses) to one of the other members of the trio whose job it is to pay attention and to listen. The third person has to disrupt the communication in whatever way she chooses. The game continues for perhaps two minutes. Then everyone changes role, with say the interrupter becoming the speaker, the listener becoming the interrupter, and the speaker becoming the listener. After another two minutes the roles are changed again, so that everyone has had a turn in each part.

This game dramatizes a frequent situation in groups, and in life: two people with something going on between them and a third, apparently excluded and wanting to break it up – or does she just slink away? Freud named this negotiation of three-person relationships the Oedipal conflict, and thought it central to entrance into adulthood.

In the group approach, issues such as these are enacted in quasi-fantasy, game-like form. Nothing need be said about parents, about rivalry or jealousy. When playing the game, if one throws oneself into it as interrupter, one both is excluded (the rules of the game say so) and one finds oneself thinking and feeling things about the exclusion and how to end it, or perhaps about how one might just give up, or say to oneself 'I don't want to play these silly games'. One is both playing and not playing. The thoughts and feelings one has may be generated in an artificial situation, but it is hard to claim that they are not one's own thoughts and feelings.

It is on this boundary between playing and reality that therapy occurs, both in one-to-one settings and in groups. Dramas of trust and distrust or of Oedipal conflicts occur in both settings. In interpretive individual therapy the therapist's job is to recognize the interpersonal structure of what is going on, and bring it into play. In groups, on the other hand, it is often enacted in the form of a playful metaphor, rather than being interpreted. In groups the play takes place perhaps reluctantly, perhaps hammily, perhaps with abandonment; but in taking part in it the person can gain access to disowned aspects of herself, now made more acceptable.

The culture of a group

Most group leaders would think it inappropriate simply to rehearse a group through a set of encounter games. If they encouraged games, they would allow them to grow out of what was happening in the group. For the trust game to be offered when a group was reticent, distrustful or the members unwilling to make much contact together, might be appropriate. Similarly if a pattern emerged that whenever a certain person was speaking somebody else would change the subject, the leader might say to the person interrupted, 'I've noticed that every time you start talking, someone takes the group's attention away from you.' Or alternatively she might say, 'I've got a game I'd like to suggest', and ask the group to divide into threes and play the interruption game. In either case it is unlikely that the subsequent pattern of interaction will be as rigid as before. It may recur throughout the life of the group, but with each drawing of attention to its relational qualities, the members of the group might acquire a quantum of choice, rather than their usual impossibility to do anything different.

Partly this changing of patterns comes about from creating a group culture in which it becomes all right for certain things to go on in the group. After one person has spoken openly about something that concerns her, it has become a negotiated part of the group's culture that speaking openly can go on. Once the trust game which involves some bodily contact has occurred, or once somebody has hugged somebody else, then that can go on too. It is part of popular knowledge of encounter groups that people who go to such groups both talk about feelings and become less inhibited about touching each other. As if to underline the difference with ordinary western behaviour, groups are sometimes called 'touchy-feely groups' or even more scathingly 'group gropes'.

Whatever one thinks about such activities, a group is a place where there is the opportunity to create a new culture. Just as children will create new games out of existing situations and materials, so from the partial vacuum of there being very few rules, a group creates the possibilities of new rules and customs of interaction among its members, a new ethos on a cultural island.

It does this in a number of ways. First, groups are usually held away from familiar settings, for example at a residential centre. Secondly, the usual cues for interaction are stripped down to a minimum, or are even given a push in a slightly unexpected direction. So the circle of cushions on a floor of a room without furniture is a clear non-verbal signal that the ordinary accompaniments of group meetings, that is chairs, desks, blackboards and lecterns are not to be the furniture of this new culture. Only cushions are arranged in a circle to imply that people will talk to each other with no clear marks of status. Of course once a person has been to one group of this kind, these arrangements themselves become part of a familiar furniture.

The refusal of a leader to take too much part in the early interactions, and to abdicate immediately from the role of setter of an agenda, or judge of what should or should not happen, is part of the same notion.

It is under these circumstances that the group might have the best chance of generating its own culture, and its own story of its meetings. Such experiences are creative and often moving and exhilarating. This of course does not mean that each group is completely idiosyncratic, any more than is children's play. What it does mean is that the potentiality for play, and for playfulness, and the possibilities of creativity, and of spontaneity are increased, and the obligations of rigidity and repetition decreased.

Neither does it mean that the play is without seriousness. It becomes engaging just in so far as it touches people's most heartfelt concerns, as anyone who watches or can remember children's play will know.

A drama unfolds

As the group which Emma attended went on, she found herself enjoying it. The leader said something about how initially people had been wary. They now seemed more open. Emma realized that this was why she felt less bored. A woman called Jane talked about a relationship she was in, and how she seemed to have reached exactly the same place with this man as she had with her husband from whom she was now divorced. She talked about how he irritated her, and said she found herself restlessly seeking excitement with someone else. In fact, she said, she had been sitting in the group feeling hypocritical that the real reason she had come was to see if there was someone here that she fancied, but there was not.

Emma was fascinated and shocked. Fascinated that she could recognize in herself some of the things that this woman was talking about. She felt warmly towards her while she was speaking. But shocked that she should have said that she was coming here to pick someone up, and that she had said so. Emma thought the men in the group must have felt rejected. She thought that she would not have been brave enough to say such a thing, and suddenly had an image of her friend Eileen talking about being 'upfront'.

Other people in the group evidently too felt moved by what Jane had said. Some wanted to talk about how difficult sexual relationships always were. One woman said she was a lesbian, and felt that for her sexual relationships with women were the only ones that stood any chance. But Jane said no, it wasn't that. She felt there was something wrong with her, and burst into tears. Emma felt an impulse to go and sit next to Jane, and maybe offer her a handkerchief, but decided that was not really possible. She was somewhat surprised to see the leader Christine go and do exactly what she had been thinking of. She linked her arm companionably in Jane's. Jane and Christine were saying something to each other, which Emma could not quite hear, but it seemed to be all right just to sit there while this was going on. In the end Jane said she felt quite a bit better, and glad she had cried.

There was another silence, but Emma felt it had a different quality to the one at the beginning of the group. It was difficult to name, but it seemed calmer.

It was Christine the leader who broke it by asking one of the members, James, 'What are you feeling? You seem to be quite a long way away.' Emma had seen that James seemed to sit rather hunched up, and not looking at anyone, but had not taken much notice of him. She felt immediately guilty that she should have said something to him.

James said he couldn't say anything since he felt that though other people seemed to enjoy the group, he was not feeling part of it. Christine was quite right, he was feeling a long way away, and thought it had been a mistake to come.

Christine asked, 'Is there anything you would like to do about that?' James grinned a bit and said, 'Well I'm glad you noticed.'

Christine laughed and said, 'I could scarcely avoid noticing', and moved herself back out of the circle a little way, hunched her shoulders, and stared at the ground in a caricature of the way James had been sitting throughout most of the group. Emma wondered whether this wasn't a bit cruel of Christine, but felt that she had done it without malice. James laughed too, and said, 'I think you are right . . . suppose I was wanting to be noticed, but I can't seem to help it, I just feel out of place here. Everyone else seems to be able to talk about themselves, and I don't feel I can do that.'

Christine replied that she supposed that sitting like that was precisely his way of saying what he wanted to, and that she appreciated him saying that he felt rather wary of the rest of the group. She imagined there were other people here who felt rather similarly. Three people said they did, but had not been able to say so. Christine, continuing to talk to James, said, 'I've a suggestion about something we could all do together, which I wonder if you would like to try.' She briefly described the trust game. James agreed and had the first go at falling in the middle. After a few goes of moving his feet as he fell, he let himself go, and seemed to enjoy himself. 'Getting into it', Emma thought her friend Eileen would have said.

Several people had a go in the middle, including Emma who found the falling through space to be caught by confident arms, and pushed gently back towards the other side of the circle, rather exciting, or at least a mixture of exciting and safe. 'This', she supposed, 'was "Getting into it".' She also found herself thinking about where one of the members of the circle, Ian, was standing, and thought she could recognize him as she fell.

The game ended with people laughing as someone crumpled into a heap instead of letting himself fall towards the circle. James talked about how he felt that people did not like him, and seemed surprised when some people said one or two rather specific things that they did like. Soon afterwards the group broke for supper. Emma found herself going with Ian. Over supper they compared notes about the group. Emma felt she'd found a friend and ally in the group.

Later in the evening Emma told the group how she had come because she often felt depressed and did not know at all why, except that she felt that things in her relationship with her husband Tom seemed much flatter than they used to be. Tom was always working, and though he was not unkind, somehow seemed more interested in the computers with which he worked than in her. Emma talked rather haltingly, and then was appalled to hear herself saying, 'We used to make love quite a lot, but now Tom always seems preoccupied, and so we don't much any more, and I feel quite relieved that we don't have to.'

Ian, who was sitting next to her, placed his hand on hers quite gently. She felt grateful for his understanding. Other people in the group too spoke to her sympathetically, and she felt that maybe it was all right to have said what she did, though she felt sure she would regret it later. It seemed so revealing, and a bit disloyal.

Towards the end of the evening, Ian was talking about how difficult he found school, and that he found his relationships with pupils upsetting because he would like to be able to get to know them better, but that keeping discipline, the syllabus and examinations made that impossible. He had been thinking about whether he might train as a counsellor and give up teaching, which was partly why he'd come to the group. He seemed to speak mostly to the leader Christine. Emma felt a bit put out that he wasn't talking to her. But she quickly put the thought aside.

The woman who had said she was a lesbian suggested that next day everyone bring some food to share for lunch. And everyone went home.

Emma went back to stay with her friend Eileen, feeling both excited and confused. The group had not been nearly as bad as she had expected. She did, however, find her thoughts racing: thinking that she shouldn't have said what she did about Tom and her, finding that Ian kept coming into her mind, as someone who seemed very capable and sensitive, thinking, 'Oh dear this is what happens in these groups, they just provide an emotional hothouse for people who are feeling dissatisfied with their lives, so they start fancying new people!'

When she got back, Eileen was eager to talk about the group. But Emma found herself not wanting to say much, except she was glad she had gone, and that she was quite impressed with the leader who seemed to be able to make things happen in an unobtrusive way, and without being bossy.

She went to bed, but couldn't fall asleep, as her thoughts were still racing, thinking about what she and the others had said in the group, about Ian, and Tom, about Christine. Finally she slept.

The next day Christine suggested the group start by people telling each other anything that they had left undone from the day before. People talked. One man said he felt angry with the lesbian woman for bringing sexual politics into it. Another said that he had felt quite rejected when Jane had said she didn't fancy any of the men here, and although there wasn't any reason why she should fancy him, he still felt it was a bit of a put-down.

Later in the morning, Ian started talking about how he had been thinking quite a lot about the group, and wanted to say that he felt he had been living under false pretences. He had a child with Downs Syndrome, and he had never really got over the shock of that. He thought in some ways he did love his little boy, but often he felt he didn't. What was worse was that the person who was most important to him in all the world, his wife, had devoted herself to the child, and somehow set such a standard that he felt he couldn't live up to it. The talk spiralled off about Ian, his wife and their child. Emma found herself feeling more and more detached. She hadn't thought that Ian was married. She'd wondered, but concluded that he probably wasn't. She felt quite let down. For no good reason, of course. But she felt rather withdrawn from things for the rest of the morning, from the intensity that other people seemed to be engaged in, and from the pleasure of sharing lunch together. But she went through the motions with a good grace.

In the middle of the afternoon, after they had had a break for tea, Christine said, 'Would everyone just pause for a moment, and ask themselves what they have *not* been saying in this group?' Emma found herself thinking that what she wasn't saying, and certainly wasn't going to say, was that she was feeling disappointed. It wasn't the group's fault. Everyone else seemed to be getting a lot out of it. It was her own fault. It wasn't really her sort of thing.

People started going round the circle saying some things that they hadn't been saying, though Emma noticed that some people didn't join in, and felt relieved, but at the same time rather coerced by this ritual. But in the middle of her thoughts Ian said, directly to her, 'I wonder what you are thinking, Emma? I thought you liked me yesterday, but today since I talked about my son you've been very cold and distant.'

Emma said, 'Oh no, I do like you, I've not felt cold towards you.'

Christine said, 'I've been wondering why you seem withdrawn too, and thinking about what you were saying yesterday, about how with your husband, was it Tom? . . . you find yourself checking out, and just going through the motions. It sounded to me as if you were quite disappointed in him, and I'm wondering if you are disappointed with us too.'

Emma hastened to say, 'No . . . at least I don't think so. It's just that I don't think this kind of thing is for me.' And then to Ian, 'I suppose I thought you liked me when we had supper last night. But I suppose the thing is that this morning I thought perhaps that I'd been wrong, and that you just had lunch with me because . . . I don't know, probably just because I was standing there. I can see you've got a lot on your mind your school, your counselling course, your son, your wife.'

'And so you just felt like checking out, and going through the motions until it was time to go home', said Christine. Emma wasn't sure that Christine was on about. That was the second time she had said that and it was irritating. After a pause Christine said, 'May I suggest something? Could you come over here and sit opposite Ian, but imagine he is your husband Tom, and tell him some of the things you find disappointing about him.'

Emma was reluctant, but felt somehow that the group would think she was a coward if she didn't try. She sat opposite Ian, and very pointedly calling him Tom started saying she was fed up with him working so much, she resented him having something which seemed so much more important than her, particularly when he knew that she didn't have anything that important in her life, that she felt he was bored with her. Ian/Tom responded equably, saying that he wasn't bored, that he was interested but that he did have a lot to do at the moment, and was sorry. But then surprisingly said, 'But you are so hard to reach. You become quite untouchable. I thought you just wanted to be left alone.'

'Are you being Ian or Tom when you say that?' demanded Emma.

'Well . . . either I suppose. You seem to become very, very aloof, quite unreachable.'

Emma found her head reeling slightly. Feeling both sad and pensive, as she sensed how close what she was feeling about Ian and the group was to how she felt about Tom and her relationship with him.

Christine said, 'It's as if something had been agreed between you, but then you feel terribly hurt that it didn't happen, and need to protect yourself.'

Emma felt a pang that this was probably quite right, both about her disappointment, and how she made sure she would stay disappointed by not really being there any more. She stared at the floor. She felt Christine come over, to put her arm round her, and also felt Ian's hand on her foot, quite comfortingly.

Aloof! Aloof? Emma had never thought of herself as aloof, she had thought of herself as rather too available to everyone, and rather patient. But she realized that this was not exactly right. She did sometimes make herself absolutely unavailable.

There was a long silence, again for Emma quite different from the other silences there had been in the group. She looked at Ian. 'I think I'd been expecting something of you that you hadn't really given me any reason to expect', she said. 'I've been feeling very unattractive recently, and though I don't want to start anything, I liked it when you asked me to lunch. I'm sorry about your little boy – it must be difficult, but though you think you're not much good for him I think he's lucky to have you as a daddy.'

Emma went home feeling much more hopeful about things than

she had been doing, and looking forward to talking to Tom. Though she felt somewhat confused by some of the things that had gone on, looking back she realized she had enjoyed it, that it had somehow been a privilege to feel so close to people, and that she now felt rather high.

But is this more than a post-group glow after an engaging experience? Do groups do more than provide a form of participatory theatre with non-professional actors?

7

The effects of groups

There is a substantial body of work enquiring empirically into the effects of groups. Some of the results seem less clear than for individual therapy, partly because most of the people who go to groups do not complain explicitly of symptoms, which can be measured relatively easily. Rather they go for reasons of personal growth or exploration, and the measures taken are typically of the extent to which they or others perceive that they have achieved this. The literature on outcomes of group therapy with symptomatic clients will not be treated here because many of the types of therapy involved are simply group adaptations of individual therapy, rather than distinctively group participation as described in the last chapter. The usefulness of groups in clinical settings is reviewed by P.B. Smith *et al.* (1980), and overall the mean effect size in M.L. Smith *et al.*'s (1980) meta-analysis was 0.83 of a standard deviation for group psychotherapy, remarkably similar to the overall mean effect size for individual therapy of 0.87.

Lieberman, Yalom and Miles's study

As in chapter 5 where the effects of individual therapy were discussed, in this chapter first a single study, generally thought to be one of the best that has been done, will be presented, as a paradigm. Then to illustrate the range of results in the area, a review of the literature will be described.

The piece of empirical work which seems to have been most influential in evaluating sensitivity and encounter groups was Lieberman, Yalom and Miles's (1973) *Encounter Groups: First Facts*.

In this substantial and informative book, the benefits and harm from a group experience were studied in 206 students of Stanford University, California, as were the characteristics of the leaders of the groups. Each student volunteer was assigned by the researchers to one of eighteen different groups which met for thirty hours. A large number of measures was taken. One set was of the individual's own ratings before, immediately after and six months after the group. Further measures of the amount of learning and change that each participant had achieved were taken from the group leaders, other group participants and from friends.

Ten different styles of group were included in the study, including T-groups, psychodrama groups, a psychoanalytic group, various other kinds of encounter and growth groups, and two that ran without leaders but with the benefit of a tape recorder and some 'encounter tapes'.

The groups were run by professional group leaders, each experienced in one of the approaches which were included. The leaders were mostly psychiatrists and psychologists, and they were chosen by the researchers who asked professionals to select from a list of sixty leaders the two best in the Bay area who worked in the style that they were familiar with.

The main measures of the style of leadership and the atmosphere in each of the groups were assessed from ratings made by a team of twenty-nine trained clinicians who acted as non-participant observers. Every group session was attended for three hours by two observers, who made independent ratings, and were rotated among the groups and among different pairings of observers. In addition, participants rated both the leaders and their own overall experience of the groups.

The main outcome measures which Lieberman *et al.* used were composite scores which determined whether on balance each of the participants benefited or otherwise from their experience in the group. Those who benefited most were called 'high learners'. These were people who had a 'highly constructive experience in the group the effects of which were still apparent six months later' (p. 184). There were fifteen of these, 7.3 per cent of the total.

The finding from this study that received the most public attention was that groups sometimes led to 'casualties'. This term was used by Lieberman *et al.* for people at the other end of their scale of outcome who 'as a direct result of [their] experience in the encounter group, became more psychologically distressed and/or employed more maladaptive mechanisms of defence' (p. 171). Sixteen people (7.8 per cent) were considered to have become casualties.

Casualties in groups

Casualties were people who felt subsequently that the group had harmed them, or that they had suffered from excessively negative feelings about themselves. In some cases casualties had quite severe breakdowns which the researchers thought had been prompted or exacerbated by the group.

The distribution of casualties among the groups was not uniform: six groups had no casualties, whereas four of the groups had more than one casualty, and three of these high-risk groups had leaders whose style was 'characterized by high aggressive stimulation, high charisma, high individual focus, high support and high confrontation' (p. 174).

These findings, of course, mesh closely with some public reservations and alarm about groups and groupies. Now, in the 1980s, the fashionable surge of encounter groups is past. Groups, growth centres and humanistic therapies have become both less of a boom industry, and more assimilated to respectable pursuits of professional training, counselling and therapy. Alarm has somewhat subsided, although some reservations remain that some irresponsible and exploitative leaders are involved, and that the heightened emotional experience amplified by group pressures can be either psychiatrically dangerous, or subvert the individual's more rational belief systems.

Some of these reservations may be perfectly appropriate, and Lieberman *et al.*'s book brings some of them into focus. It seems best to discuss the issue in two stages, first the degree to which the alarm over casualties is exaggerated, and secondly the extent to which in groups, as in individual therapy, harm can be done.

First the exaggeration: Lieberman *et al.*'s study although purporting to purvey the first 'facts' is not methodologically very adequate on this subject of casualties. Several of the people who were casualties had been feeling fragile or insecure before the group, and went to the group as a means of dealing with long-standing problems. Groups may be 'therapy for normals', but it is also known that people who are feeling upset are more likely to go to groups. Thus it is difficult to be sure whether the casualties are caused by the groups, or whether groups attract a high proportion of people who are fragile or feel bad about themselves.

One of the tasks of a research study, and one of the values of control subjects in an experiment, is to sort out what factors are responsible for each kind of effect. In the study of Sloane *et al.* (1975) on the outcome of individual therapy, which was discussed in chapter 5, candidates for therapy were randomly assigned by the researchers to either one of the therapy conditions or to a waiting list, and the people on the waiting list for therapy were the control group. This procedure contributed to making Sloane *et al.*'s study such a good one, and one from which it is possible to draw conclusions about the effectiveness of therapy as such. Lieberman *et al.* did not use any comparable procedure. They did include a set of controls: sixty-nine students matched with the group participants, but who did not take part in the groups. These controls were chosen from people interested in groups, who had *not* volunteered to go to a group in this study.

The researchers thus let two opportunities pass. First by not randomly assigning people who had volunteered, either to a group or to some procedure such as the promise of a group in a month's time, they made it impossible to discover whether the group experience as such had increased the rate of casualty in the kinds of people who volunteer for groups. Secondly by failing to investigate possible casualty status in the control subjects they had chosen, they deprived readers of any idea of what rates of psychological casualty predominated among undergraduates who did not attend a group.

The authors detected casualties by investigating group participants who gave cause for most concern. These were about half the total, and cause for concern was generated in various ways including members' own responses to the group experience, responses from the leaders, from friends, and from the reports of other members to such questions as, 'Can you think of people in your group who were hurt by the experience?' (p. 171). Eight months after the group each of these casualty suspects who could be reached was interviewed for fifteen or twenty minutes by phone to see if any loss of self-esteem, decrease in interpersonal functioning and so on was reported. If suspicion that the person might be a casualty was increased he was given an in-depth interview in person or by telephone. On the basis of these enquiries the researchers decided both who was a casualty, and whether the casualty was directly caused by the group.

Other research studies of group outcome have failed to detect casualties in such high proportions. For instance P.B. Smith (1975) using Lieberman *et al.*'s technique of asking other group members who they thought might be a casualty, examined casualty suspects among members of week-long groups and found no casualties. In a study by Bebout and Gordon (1972) going on at the University of California campus at Berkeley at the same time as Lieberman *et al.*'s at Stanford, comments from only 2.9 per cent of 680 participants could be considered evidence of casualty status.

As Smith (1975) points out, groups may occasionally be harmful, but so are other aspects of life. Taking examinations, getting married, applying for jobs or having individual therapy also carry a risk of adverse effects. Harmful effects, moreover, may have multiple reasons, therefore Lieberman *et al.*'s procedure of discovering which members of the study had become a casualty as a 'direct' result of the group is questionable.

It would be absurd to suppose that anything which had long-lasting or profound effects, for example education, marriage, employment (or refusal of employment) and therapy could only be benign, much though educators, spouses, employers and therapists would like this. It is not clear from available research findings that groups are more risky that other things that people choose to do in our society. In this context the supposition that encounter groups are about as dangerous as being brainwashed is much exaggerated.

This does not however negate the possibility that harm is done in groups, or shelve the question of how it might be minimized by leaders, or guarded against by participants.

Styles of leadership

Lieberman *et al*.'s work indicated that the leaders most likely to do harm were those who were either what they call energizers, charismatic, unpredictable people who stimulated the group and made things happen, or impersonal, *laissez-faire* leaders who did not provide enough input or direction.

Six of the sixteen casualties said they felt personally attacked by the leader, four felt damaging attacks from other members and three others felt rejected. Other casualties had rather unrealistic expectations of the group, or felt that they were not able to live up to the group's standards. An overall sense of the people described as casualties is either that they had felt exposed and attacked or that they felt worthless, and that the group had then left them in this state without any resources for coping with these feelings.

These are important findings, and they raise a proper concern for what kinds of people might be suitable as group leaders, for what kinds of training and/or selection is appropriate and perhaps more importantly for what to look out for when one is contemplating going to a group.

Lieberman *et al.* summarize their findings by saying that while some of the groups they studied were highly productive learning environments, others were on balance destructive. Their conclusion echoes a finding of Truax and Mitchell (1971) on individual therapists. Whereas about a third of therapists seem successful and are on average able to make some beneficial difference for their clients, some are ineffective, while some are 'psychonoxious' and are on balance harmful.

A clear example of a comparison between two individual therapists who seem to have had quite different effects is given by Bergin (1971). He presents the examples of two therapists, called A and B. They worked for several years with boys who, during their childhood and early adolescence, attended a well-known clinical centre. The study was carried out by analysing the clinic's case notes, and by investigating the psychiatric status of the children in adulthood. The children were all severely disturbed when they attended the clinic and, according to the notes, at the time of starting therapy there were no systematic differences between the cases seen by A and those seen by B. However, at follow-up in adulthood, of fifteen people seen by A, six were well and functioning adequately. Four had been hospitalized at some time with a diagnosis of schizophrenia. Of the thirteen people seen by B none was functioning adequately, and eleven had been hospitalized with diagnoses of schizophrenia.

The styles of the two therapists relate to some of Lieberman *et al.*'s remarks about their group leaders. Therapist A devoted more time to cases that later turned out to be more disturbed, B did the opposite. A was obviously interested in the boys, liked and respected them, and helped them in building up ways of coping with the world, B seemed to move 'more precipitously into presumably deep material'. The author of the anonymous report cited by Bergin, concludes that the children

> were already experiencing nearly intolerable degrees of anxiety, vulnerability . . . and isolated alienation. When the therapist increased these feelings without being at the same time able to help the boy develop ways of coping with them, he may well have played a part in subsequent psychotic developments. (Bergin, 1971, p. 251)

This result is extreme, and Bergin may be wrong in his analysis. The children seen by B might have grown up disabled anyway. Although it is highly likely that A was a good therapist, B might just have been ineffective, rather than actively harmful.

Though Lieberman *et al.* argue that some groups do people harm, the harm which they supposed to accrue from their groups was very mild compared with the outcome for B's patients in the study reported by Bergin.

There is a common thread though. One danger of therapy or groups may be to expose delicate areas in which defences exist which may not be ideal, but have at least served the purpose of keeping people psychologically protected from what they feel to be dangerous. Most therapy can be seen as the destructuring of certain rigid and/or maladaptive defence systems or strategies, along with the possibility of developing better ways of coping with those things which were being defended against (see for example Ryle, 1982).

The building of more appropriate coping strategies can best take place in an atmosphere of support. It seems likely that though psychonoxious therapists or group leaders may be good at attacking defences, they fail in not providing the necessary accompanying support. It may be that although this kind of experience for vulnerable people either in individual therapy or groups is risky, the risk in a group may be not be so great because of the lesser dependency. Although the size of the risk may be smaller, it may be more frequent, because people often simply turn up for a group, take part in it, and then leave. The possibility of them not having had a proper amount of attention, and of having to deal with tumultuous feelings without support, is increased.

The impression that some therapists are effective, and others not, was strongly emphasized by Lieberman *et al.* They took a large number of measures from their non-participant observers of the leaders' behaviour patterns. They classified these to see which were related to good, bad and indifferent outcomes of the groups.

The leaders of groups in which the most participants benefited, but without high incidence of casualties, were those who provided a moderate level of stimulation in an atmosphere of caring, and a high level of 'meaning attribution'. Caring was assessed by the degree to which leaders offered friendship, warmth and support, and meaning attribution by the extent to which leaders provided conceptualizations for what was going on either in terms of group interaction, or at the individual level.

Thus, in the story of Ms Emma H's visit to a group in the previous chapter, the leader Christine would have been seen by observers to be providing caring by offering support and friendship to Jane, James and Emma, and by her encouragement of members to seek feedback from others.

She would also have scored highly on 'meaning attribution'. She made sense of the interactive issues of the whole group when near the beginning she talked about what had been going on in terms of defensive metaphors of 'fencing' and 'manoeuvres', later attributed this to wariness, and contrasted it with interpersonal openness. Christine made a more elaborate attribution of meaning of an individual kind in suggesting that Emma's withdrawals had to do with feeling hurt and disappointed.

In talking to James about how he seemed to be left out of the group, she both made sense of an implied group dynamic of allowing James to become an outsider, and made the individual interpretation to him. It is usually a significant event when any participant becomes very deviant from the evolving group culture, without seeking to affect the way it is evolving. P.B. Smith (1980a) suggests that at the end of each session leaders should think about each group member in turn, asking themselves whether and in what ways they feel worried about each person.

Benefits of groups

The measures made by Lieberman *et al.* were ratings from participants themselves, from leaders, from co-participants and from members of the person's social network. They were grouped into six areas: values, behaviour, self-regard, conceptions of others, various perspectives on the amount of change, and follow-up ratings from members of the person's social network. The researchers present the overall results of their study in terms of a composite measure arrived at by discussing each participant in turn and assigning him to one of five overall outcome categories (indicated by single quotation marks in this paragraph). Of those who started the groups approximately one-third benefited substantially as assessed immediately after the group. At this time 14 per cent were 'high learners' who had positive changes usually on five out of the six areas indicated above; and 19 per cent were 'moderate changers', who made predominantly positive changes, with few or no negative changes. People who were 'unchanged' either showing no appreciable changes, or gains and losses which were judged by the researchers to be about equal, accounted for 38 per cent of participants. There were 8 per cent of 'moderate negative changers' showing predominantly negative changes, 8 per cent were 'casualties', and 13 per cent dropped out before the end of their group.

Of the people who benefited three-quarters had retained this benefit at the follow-up interview 6–8 months after the group, though only about 10 per cent who had showed no benefit immediately afterwards showed benefit at follow-up, indicating that 'late blooming' after a group is not common.

These composite measures contrasted rather sharply with the leaders' estimates that about 90 per cent of the members had benefited in some way, and that 30 per cent of them had benefited very considerably. This finding, that therapists' and group leaders' assessments are considerably more optimistic than those derived from any other source, has now become a common one in all types of outcome assessment. It emphasizes the value of assessments other than simply asking therapists and group leaders whether they thought their clients did well.

The views of the participants themselves were also rather more optimistic than Lieberman *et al.*'s combined indices, although there might be good reason for taking them more seriously than the therapists' assessments. Of those who completed the groups 78 per cent thought the experience constructive and 61 per cent thought they had learned a great deal. Overall it seems likely that the best estimate of benefit is probably somewhere between the researchers' very conservative estimate, of about one-third of the members benefiting substantially, and the participants' estimates that rather over a half did so.

The most valuable indices in research such as this should be comparisons with the control subjects. Despite the inadequacy of the control group, which means that the reader should maintain some degree of reservation, statistically significant differences were reported between participants and controls. These included for the participants as compared with controls: increased positive attitude to groups and to the concept of growing and changing, more adequate and more considerate behaviour towards others, and coping strategies becoming more active rather than passive. All these differences between participants and controls had decreased by follow-up, though the difference was still statistically significant for the adequacy of behaviour towards others.

The most common type of change in those who benefited was an increased openness to others. People were more honest with each other, and were somewhat relieved to find that on balance the consequences of being more direct both inside and outside the group were beneficial rather than disastrous. In so far as the strategy of personal concealment is defensive, and perhaps more appropriate to childhood than adulthood, then it is easy to see how this effect is exactly along the lines expected by most psychotherapeutic theory.

Ten of the fifteen high learners also came out of the group with enhanced self-esteem. Rather than fearing that others did not like them, they felt more liked, and more likeable. Overall they felt less concerned about carefully maintaining a protective front, since they now felt they had a more solid sense of themselves, less subject to what they imagined were others' derogatory judgements of them. They felt more able to be themselves, and therefore able to take more risks. This again seems an aspect of the reduction of defensiveness, or of what Rogers (1961) would describe as an increase in congruence.

Other areas in which high learners made changes were in taking responsibility for themselves, and their own feelings, greater acceptance of others, and coping with upsets and dilemmas in direct ways rather than by denial or other evasive tactics.

An important contribution of Lieberman *et al.*'s book is that it combines statistical comparisons with evocative case material. One gets the sense of some of the people from this study having turned an important corner in their life: not that they now cope with complete 'maturity', but that the group acted as the occasion for an important change of direction, which was still maintained 6–8 months later.

In terms of the story in the previous chapter, if Emma were to maintain the sense that she used a disowned tactic of withdrawal as a way of coping with disappointments, and succeeded in speaking, for instance to Tom, about the ways in which she felt disappointed by him, then these would be the kinds of changes that groups seek to provide the occasion for, and researchers try to detect. If Emma felt positive towards the group, felt the changes she had made were valuable, and if other members of the group, the leader, and the members of her social network such as Tom her husband and Eileen her friend were to notice them, and they were maintained for six months, then she would be the sort of person who Lieberman *et al.* might classify as a high learner.

Smith's review of group outcome studies

Important though it was, Lieberman, Yalom and Miles's study left several issues unresolved. What are the results on outcome in trials with proper control groups? How do groups such as encounter groups and sensitivity groups which are not explicitly designated as psychotherapy groups compare with ones that are? What kinds of factors might make for changes that are beneficial and lasting rather than simply pleasant and ephemeral? What kinds of leadership behaviour or style are indicated?

P.B. Smith (1980a, 1980b) has reviewed the findings of approximately one hundred published studies of group experience and sensitivity training which fulfil the criterion of comparing people who participated in a group that lasted for at least twenty hours, with control subjects who did not attend a group. Instead of considering the results in terms of people who underwent particular kinds of change, he considered how many studies which used each kind of measure showed a benefit for those attending the group, as compared with the controls.

For instance on global measures of self-concept, in which people are asked whether they feel more or less favourable towards themselves than at the initial assessment, Smith found forty-four studies, in which twenty-one found significantly greater changes for people who attended groups. Only nine of the studies included follow-up measures, but in six of these the enhanced self-concept persisted. In studies that investigated more specific measures of self-concept, ten out of twenty-four found increased sense of the self as an effective agent, ten out of twelve found increased open-mindedness, and sixteen out of twenty-four showed increased orientation towards participation.

Smith also reviewed a set of studies which measured the behaviour of people who had attended groups, as perceived by others. Seventeen out of twenty-six studies of interpersonal communication and performance found positive changes for group members. As an example, Pfister (1975) found that members of the public making 'non-adversive' contacts with police who had attended a sensitivity training group found them warmer, more understanding, and more willing to act as if they and the citizen were co-workers facing common problems, than control police who had not been to a group.

After attending groups people tend to feel more autonomous and self-accepting, and less defensive. In interpersonal behaviour they tend to be more aware and accepting of the other person. These kinds of change are among the goals of T-groups, sensitivity groups, encounter groups and the like, so the finding that they are quite frequently detected in controlled empirical studies is encouraging for the proponents of groups. Studies less often include follow-up of effects six months or a year later, and when they do, although there is some persistence, there is usually a decline in the magnitude of effect. This decline also occurs after individual therapy.

Smith concludes that the weight of evidence is that groups do produce beneficial changes in the directions corresponding to the goals of group work. What is not clear simply from studying the empirical evidence is whether one should see these changes as large or small, as important or unimportant. Lieberman *et al.* remain cautious, and argue that though positive changes associated with groups are clearly demonstrable, they are smaller than those associated with psychotherapy.

What they mean by this is not entirely clear. They make the important point that groups became popular because they were for many people, fun. But having emotional excitement, or feelings of interpersonal warmth, is not the same as achieving personal learning or change.

The empirical evidence does not allow a completely straightforward decision as to whether encounter groups are better at what they set out to achieve than therapy is at what it sets out to achieve, since the measures are often different. The best evidence is from M.L. Smith *et al.*'s (1980) meta-analysis of the outcomes of therapy. The therapies they call 'verbal' which include the humanistic sensitivity and encounter practices described here, produce effect sizes on normals as large as those on neurotic and phobic clients (p. 99). Presumably many of the measures in question are of aspects like self-esteem, which, as M.L. Smith *et al.* show, the humanistic therapies such as Rogers's and the groups described here are good at producing.

The question as to what makes for longer-lasting effects in groups is clearly an important one, and will be taken up in the next chapter. Here it needs to be pointed out that groups do tend to induce a post-group glow, and though this is not in any sense a bad thing it should not be mistaken for long-term changes. In social psychological terms the issue is that of generalization. What kinds of experiences in groups can one take outside the group: home to one's life with friends and relations, or to work with one's colleagues.

Finally it seems clear that the specific school in which a therapist or group leader works, for example Rogerian, psychoanalytic, T-group, and so on is less important for outcome than his style of working. This is one of the themes of this book. It emerged in M.L. Smith *et al*.'s meta-analysis. It emerged again in the study of Lieberman *et al*. too, in which it was found that what was most important was not the type of group, but the degree to which the leader provided the emotional stimulation, caring and meaning attribution. The terms in which the meaning attribution was made seemed less important for the participants.

As in individual practice, the therapeutic theory employed is primarily of importance for the therapist or leader. For the client, much more important is the therapist's actual abilities to take part in warm and straightforward relationships with his clients, while also remaining separate, both giving them support and making sense of what goes on.

8

Personal learning in groups

An implication of Lieberman, Yalom and Miles's book was that two fundamental issues in groups are what the leader is up to, and what kinds of groups might provide a good learning environment. These are the subjects of this chapter.

A group leader has a very different kind of influence than a committee chairperson, a teacher or a priest. Groups take on a life of their own, and it is part of the leader's function to enable them to do so. Particularly at the start of a group, the leader has a distinctive role. She has more potential influence than anyone else on whether the group is a constructive experience for its participants. However much the ideology of groups is non-authoritarian, and based on a cultural norm of every member being responsible for herself, this state of affairs does not necessarily come about by accident. At the same time, personal and interpersonal responsibility cannot be prescribed. It can only be discovered. The leader is responsible for helping to create a setting in which the discovery can be made.

The leader is the person most likely to have a concern that the group is a productive learning experience for *all* its participants, to have a view about what the conditions are in which that kind of experience can occur, and skills to help its occurrence.

So, without advocating any form of social engineering, we can ask the question, 'What is the role of a group leader?'

The role of a group leader

If the leader of a group does not have an agenda of items to be discussed, this does not mean that she is inactive. Part of her role is to provide the occasion and the setting for the group.

After a time the group evolves a distinctive culture, and to re-enter the group after a meal break or on a new day is to pass through what Goffman (1961) describes as the semi-permeable membrane of the group, and take part in something unique to the culture and history of that group.

A cultural island

Many group leaders prefer a group to meet for at least twenty hours for people to get to know each other, for a shared culture to evolve, and a degree of intensity to build up. Weekly meetings are rather slower than being continuously together, since it seems to take time for the group's distinctive atmosphere to develop on each occasion of meeting.

For the same reason, many group leaders favour groups which remain closed once they have been formed. People entering or leaving often disrupt the work of the group. Although such events, like every aspect of group experience, can become part of the material on which the group reflects they are often seen as distractions.

So another task that the leader has is to inform prospective members of a group that they are to commit themselves for the whole period of the group.

All these arrangements mobilize resources which add up the idea that the group takes place on a 'cultural island'. People leave their cultural mainland, cross some intervening seas, and arrive in another country, with values and customs somewhat different from their own. They enter a different ethos. As with foreign travel, part of what they are going for is the culture shock, which will give them a new sense of who they are in their own culture. The foreign land can, of course, be seductive. A person might easily feel that only here in the group she can be her true self, and experience life as it ought to be lived in its fullness and vividness.

But, of course, like the anthropologist having discovered some unspoiled tribe, whose apparent innocence or whose customs she compares favourably with the jaded and debased patterns of European or American civilization, she realizes she is a westerner. It is precisely her membership in western society that gives this other culture its sensuous appearance of difference and freshness. She must acknowledge her perspective from her own society, and she must return.

She returns, of course, not unchanged. Nor is the society to which she returns unaffected by her discoveries or her new presence. But she does return.

Much of the excitement of the movements of the 1960s and early 1970s had the sense that in the founding of encounter groups and communes, a quite new cultural order was being established. Many had longings that they might be able to go and live in groupland for ever. But as Lévi-Strauss shows after his visit to the *Tristes Tropiques* (1955), it is not so much that one form of culture is necessarily better or worse than another. Although it might be, none of us would be able to know, because we would necessarily be seeing it as children of our own particular cultural experiences. It is by experiencing the differences in culture that we can obtain a different sense of how we might be able to improve our own culture.

However urgent revolution of the slower or faster kind might be in our society, the contribution of individual therapy or groups is not that of providing an alternative and better structure of relating, though with groups that possibility looks more seductive. What is revolutionary is the possibility that the person may discover her own involvement and creative possibilities in our culture.

The leader's role is partly that of interpreter of the new ethos of the cultural island, as it evolves, partially a keeper of the emerging traditions, and partly too the person who ensures that the group has the experience of creating its own distinctive version of group culture.

Returning to the distinction made in chapter 4 about constitutive and regulative rules of a society, the traditions that the group

leader is mainly concerned with are those to do with the constitutive rules, for example that openness and directness are better
than defensiveness, a transform of course of the Freudian idea
that therapy is about making the unconscious conscious.

The acknowledged and the hidden

In groups this idea has been conceptualized rather neatly by Luft
(1963) as follows. Some of our behaviour and mental life is visible
to others in the group, while we keep other aspects hidden.
Similarly, some of our behaviour and mental life is known to
ourselves, and some hidden from us. Thus what is hidden both
from ourselves and from others, is not conscious to the life of the
group. One of the possibilities in the cultural island is to try the
personal experiment both of revealing to others more of what we
ordinarily hide from them, and asking from them perceptions of
what they can see but ordinarily do not tell us about. One of the
goals of a group might well be to increase the area of the public,
and decrease the area of the unconscious.

In Lieberman *et al.*'s study, some of the most significant and
important experiences for participants who benefited were those
where people felt the excitement and human warmth of being able
to be open, that is of not having such a large area hidden as usual.

Here for instance are two excerpts from people who Lieberman
et al. call high learners.

> I felt able to express what I felt for people in my group more fully
> than in almost any other situation I've been in. (p. 154)

Not only is self-revelation thought to be therapeutic, it is also a
liberating experience and one which, despite fears about hurting
people, or the chaos that might result, is typically accompanied by
great amounts of warmth and friendly feeling.

> Someone told me I was just 'not aware', that everything out in
> the world is not peaches and cream like I was. First it shook me
> and I felt bitter. But after more explanation, I appreciated it
> since it has made me more aware that things, objects and events
> are not always the way I picture them to be. (p. 153)

This from an upper-class black woman with a sheltered upbring-
ing, describing a perception offered to her by another participant,

enabled her to face some of the more unpleasant features of the social world which she had refused to notice.

In the group described in chapter 6 it was when people started to be self-revealing about their concerns that the group became less boring, and the fencing and manoeuvring lessened. A significant moment for Emma was when she was able to realize and tell Ian that she had been covertly expecting something of him, which he had not given her. She had become withdrawn and preoccupied, and her unspoken preoccupation had contributed to her feeling uninvolved in the group and just waiting for it to end. The leader's request for people to think of what they were not saying in the group was said with just this issue in mind, that the unspoken, and that which is supposedly being hidden from others, can nevertheless cast long shadows over both the group's interaction and individual's participation.

In that story too it was the perception of Ian, saying that he found her aloof, which both struck her and allowed her to see, with a certain amount of cathartic emotion, how she contributed to her own disappointments with people.

Part of the task of the leader is to make these kinds of experience more available, and she may do this in a number of ways, being open and self-revealing about her own feelings, by giving unjudgemental perceptions to others and so on. She may also do this more indirectly. For example she might suggest that people try the experiment in the group of using only the pronoun 'I' when talking. So someone saying 'People are always . . .' would be asked to try saying 'I am always . . .' Alternatively she might start a game in which a person sits in the middle of the group and asks other participants each to say one thing they had noticed about her.

Experiential learning

Three main kinds of learning are sanctioned in various ways by society (Oatley, 1980). In one major form, experts pass on a body of largely verbal consensual knowledge to students. A second form is the learning of skills, with a prominent component involving correct performance, and a reciprocity with the material being worked with. The third form is personal and experiential: it deals with coming to one's own knowledge of the forms of interpersonal experience, of the right ways of action in the personal domain. None of these forms is completely separable from the others. But different cultural practices emphasize the different kinds: school, the first kind, apprenticeship the second. Groups, and their emergence into both schools and industry, can be seen as a renewal of emphasis on this third kind.

Therapy, and perhaps even more strikingly, groups, draw attention to this third kind of learning. Like a skill, it is personal. It cannot be exported from person to person by speech or writing. Like a skill too it involves learning from mistakes. But the domain is not of the technical but of the personal and interpersonal world. In this kind of learning the person can only learn for herself. Whereas in the other kinds of learning there are always external criteria, a correct conceptualization, or a properly conducted performance, recognizable by teachers or craft experts. In experiential learning external criteria are not the main issue. What is learned is, as Kierkegaard (1844) said, 'inward'. On the other hand it is not exactly private. Anything but: it has profoundly to do with one's most fundamental relations with others.

This kind of learning became distinctively associated with groups as 'therapy for normals'. The primary motivation for going to a group was not to resolve symptoms, but to learn about oneself, about one's relating to others, and about the dynamics of relating in groups. These are experiential. Though a leader may attribute meanings, or encourage dramatic enactments, these matters are learned for oneself, and by one's own reflection.

Experiential learning cannot be passed on by a book, or by generalizations, and it is not a technical skill. It might be called meta-learning (cf. Bateson, 1973) in a similar term to Szasz's (1965) notion of therapy as meta-education. As well as being experiential, the 'meta' indicates that this learning is recursive or reflexive: learning about learning. One learns about one's own learning, as it has occurred in the past, making us who we are, and in present activities of taking part with others in generating the rules of the new culture of the group.

The outcome studies described in chapters 5 and 7 are attempts to investigate this kind of learning empirically, that is to say in terms of what might be reliably observed. But since the changes are experiential they rest not on external criteria, but inward ones. Indeed most schemes of measurement recognize this. They do not rely entirely on observing a person's behaviour, but on asking her, and in more sophisticated measures asking her friends, relations and associates too.

By putting the matter into the perspective of experiential learning, it becomes clear how far approaches which have to do either with external reinforcement or externally imposed social influence are from being able to address the issue. The question is not how a person can be induced to behave in particular ways, but under what kinds of circumstances can a person discover her own authenticity in relation to others.

For the therapist as well as for the client, the encounter needs to be authentic, not a set-up. This proposal echoes Rogers's criterion of the therapist needing to be genuine. The leader may mobilize resources such as arranging time and place, and by virtue of having engaged in this kind of encounter before, exercise some interpretive functions. But there need be nothing in the group setting that radically distinguishes the leader from the other members of the group. To start with she certainly has more influence, and this is important. But if by the end of the group its culture has not grown to make this redundant, then the group has been a failure, and she has merely continued to exercise this influence rather than used it.

Therapy and groups in the care of some therapists and leaders may be like the social psychological experiments in cognitive dissonance reduction, as suggested by Totman (1979, 1982), in which the clients occupy one perspective of being able to attribute their actions and their experience to themselves, while the therapist or leader attributes any changes to her influence. But such a social engineering analysis neglects the part of the therapist or leader. In so far as her participation is inauthentic, the experience of others will be flawed. Perhaps the more destructive leaders discovered by Lieberman *et al.* (1973) and described in the last chapter, might be destructive partly for this reason. They seemed to be the ones who were fond of making things happen.

Clients often suspect that therapists and group leaders are acting manipulatively, or enjoying the exercise of personal power, or are just doing a job. In so far as these are what the therapist or leader is doing, the best it is possible to imagine is that the client experience a sort of social conjuring trick. Therapy is of course a job for therapists: but if the therapist is simply going through the motions, applying formulae or technical solutions, then therapy will scarcely occur. No healing encounter between actual people is likely, because the therapist will be effectively absent. One can often hear ways in which therapists absent themselves from clients: for instance by making supposed diagnoses in a language of mild or explicit derogation designed to be withheld from the people whom it concerns: 'this person has an inadequate personality', or 'that one has a schizo-affective disorder' with the unspoken but powerful complementary implication that by contrast the therapist has not, and is well, competent and knowledgeable. To apply social engineering techniques is another manoeuvre for absenting oneself: drawing a self-protective veil over knowing oneself and preventing a relationship with the other from taking place.

Though the leader might quite properly expect people to learn and change in groups, if she does not include herself as being one of these people then her stance is questionable. Though she might have taken part in many dramas of people interacting with each other in groups, if she is not ready to take part in some more, and in the name of her own presence there, then she would be more honest to pay for a seat in the stalls of a more conventional theatre.

Safety plus challenge

One structure which both groups and individual therapy seek to provide, is a structure of simultaneous support and challenge. This apparently rather paradoxical tension is a main key to the nature of experiential therapeutic learning and helps provide an answer to the questions of the previous section. The conditions under which people might most properly make an attribution of any changes they might make to themselves, are those where first it is not personally dangerous to do so, and secondly where they have themselves perceived some good reason for making a change. The challenge need not be hostile. Nor need it be one in which the person being challenging is being bossy, or trying to get the other to do things. The person's habitual ways of acting and perceiving are challenged with the possibility of something different.

Often the challenge, as stressed by both therapeutic theory, and by Lieberman *et al.*'s survey of the important ingredients of groups, is the possibility of a new meaning emerging. This shift needs both a sense of mutuality, and the possibility of some difference emerging.

P.B. Smith (1980c) like Totman (1979, 1982) uses the attributional theory of social psychology, but with a different emphasis, to explain this structure. Therapy is about change, he proposes. It also takes place in social relationships, Therefore any change that does occur might be thought of as resulting from social influence. Following Kelman (1963) he proposes that social influence typically occurs in three main forms: compliance, identification and internalization.

Compliant actions and feelings occur when another has power in some kind of way, perhaps as a parent, a teacher or an employer. This kind of behavioural change is celebrated in behavioural theories, and in the idea of reinforcement. In using reinforcement, the other controls something we want, and is thereby able to manoeuvre aspects of our behaviour into sequences of contingency in order for us to obtain it. In addition, and in a specifically human domain of selfhood, authoritarian figures seem to be able to create resonances with the 'musts' and 'don'ts' of our internal voices, and thereby make even more likely our compliance.

Many analyses including Freud's trace psychopathology back to problems of compliance. Repression, a key term in psychoanalytic theory, is simply an intra-psychic analogy to a social relationship which produces compliance. However, though compliance is a widespread and effective form of social influence, its major experiential accompaniment according to Winnicott (1971) is a feeling of deadness, of futility. One's actions are not one's own, and there comes to seem no point in them.

With the apparent exception of one's earliest relationships, it seems that compliant behaviour does not necessarily extend much beyond the context of the person with whom one is complying. One might be polite and respectful towards one's boss to her face, but be criticizing her mercilessly when talking to one's friends. It is clear that compliance does not have much to recommend it as a social mechanism of therapy.

Identification seems more benign. It is the presumed basis for social imitations and it takes place when a person likes, or wants to be like another person. For instance a person might start to think and act in a particular kind of way, read certain kinds of books, immerse herself in particular thought patterns in order to have conversations with someone she likes or admires. In doing so she would be influenced by the other, and change through identification.

In attributional terms, if either compliance or identification occurs, one's behaviour is externally caused, and one might appropriately make an attribution external to oneself. If one's behaviour had changed because a person had power over one, then one might say, 'I did it because I had to.' If there was an identification going on, one might say, 'I did it because I hoped she would approve.'

In Kelman's third kind of social influence, which he calls internalization, although a person might derive the idea for making some kind of change from another person, or from a social situation, she makes an internal attribution. Maybe, for instance, on the occasion of some kind of challenge, or the perception of a new meaning. The person makes the change for her own reasons.

In groups, a person might find herself doing things she would not ordinarily do, perhaps talking more openly than usual. As yet, as P.B. Smith (1980c) points out, there need be no attributional dilemma. The usual external kinds of attribution can be made, for instance: 'I'm being more open because this happens to be an exceptionally friendly and trustworthy bunch of people.' But if a participant challenges someone, either directly, perhaps by giving some socially uncensored perception, or perhaps even by doing something that the observer would like to do but feels she cannot, any change she then makes is much more difficult just to disown as being externally caused.

For instance in the group of chapter 6, Ms Emma H is challenged by the leader to say some of the things she might like to say to her husband Tom, but cannot. It is suggested she says them to Ian in a role-play of the kind devised by Moreno (1940). She can, and does, attribute doing the role-play to group pressure, but in the course of doing it she experiences something new, for example the commonality of her present feelings of disappointment with other people in her life. In addition the leader suggests a new meaning for some of her feelings. She suggests that it is Emma herself who has emotionally withdrawn on these occasions. Despite this being new for her, it tallies with her own experience. She recognizes its rightness, and will be likely to make an internal attribution. She will have learned something from her own experience.

This attributional analysis has a different flavour from that on experiments in dissonance reduction. No machinery is operating noiselessly behind the scenes. Simply, a degree of apparent paradox is involved. One is more likely to learn experientially when the other is both supportive and not threatening to one's sense of self, but at the same time challenges us by being other than one expects. Neither does this require any degree of deviousness on the part of the therapist. Rather it requires a lack of some of the deviousness, and the socially sanctioned blindness to certain aspects of each other's behaviour.

Put in terms of therapy as an ethical meeting, the idea of safety plus challenge involves the creation of mutuality through shared understandings, but also the separateness of the other person. We tend to invite people either into well-understood complementary role relationships such as teacher–student, man–woman, helper–helpless, or into symmetrical patterns (Bateson, 1935): 'I'll do this to you' – 'You do the same back to me'. These structures are familiar and well-practised.

Therapy and groups offer the possibility of entering into a mutual relationship, which involves shared rules, but not necessarily the rules in which we can demand that the other person enacts a role which is complementary or symmetrical to ours. The other can be therapeutic by not being coerced into our scripts, not necessarily fitting in, but remaining separate from our image of her.

This has nothing to do with the therapist being cantankerous or contrary; these are common reactive patterns: 'I want you to do or be this' – 'No I'll do the opposite'. Rather it has to do with her both maintaining her presence with the client, *en rapport*, but being her own self.

Though in one-to-one therapy the assumption is that the client invites the therapist into old familiar patterns of transference, while the therapist paradoxically both accepts these and remains beyond their reach, in groups the theatre of possibilities widens. Everyone in the group acts as an 'other' both taking part in mutuality, and potentially unwilling just to take part in conventional patterns of interaction.

The situation both in one-to-one therapy and groups has a strong formal resemblance to the arrangements scientists choose for testing and modification of scientific theories: the laboratory and the experiment. The laboratory is a setting of safety, where potential uncontrollable consequences of actions are confined to a safe space, on a small scale. At the same time theories can be explored. The theories in question are the public ones of natural scientific knowledge. They are challenged by the possibilities of their disconfirmation.

Similarly in one-to-one therapy and groups one enters a safe space, and can experiment (cf. Oatley, 1982). T-groups with their idea of 'laboratory training' take up this same metaphor. The difference from natural science is that the theories in question are personal and practical, rather than public and natural scientific. They have to do with one's actions with others, and with the domain of *ethos*, rather than of physics.

The feelings and emotions which therapists tend to emphasize are the surprises of implicit theories being disconfirmed. In the ordinary world, such surprises can give rise to terrifying and long-lasting emotions.

Arguments and rows between members of couples, for instance, although they often feel dreadful, are one ordinary means of changing our interpersonal theories. Even faced with the unequivocal signal of having a row, we often prefer to hang on to our theories rather than change them. We might find ourselves fighting to the end in order to maintain a particular theory or some fixed idea of self, and maintaining too that 'self' is right. Therapy provides the opportunity for those feelings and emotions which signal mistakes in our interpersonal theories to lead more easily to their change than to their entrenchment. The atmosphere of safety makes it easier to let go of an old theory. The possibility that it might be challenged rather than just acceded to becomes part of the excitement of the situation rather than a danger to be avoided at all costs. Going to one-to-one therapy or a group means that we have affirmed that change itself rather than defensiveness is our intention, just as for scientists going into the laboratory means that they are prepared to have their theories affected by the world.

Withdrawing projections

The most usually reported effects of groups are that people change the ways they feel and think about themselves. However, a second group of changes occurs, in how people see, and are seen by each other.

The analogy with scientific theory is again informative. Theories are the means by which we see the world. If groups provide for the possibility of changing one's view of self because the other does not necessarily respond to an assumed expectation, at the same time they provide the possibility for a change in perception of the other.

The term usually used in therapeutic circles to describe the expectations through which we both see the other and are blinded to who she is, is projection. We project an image on to the convenient screen offered by the presence of the other person. Projections tend to occur in several layers (Oatley, 1980).

In one layer, the layer of casual interaction, we merely need to know enough to enter into conventional role relationships: teacher–student, doctor–patient, leader–led. In the group to which Ms Emma H went, some of the early activities of the group were taken up with projections of leadership roles on to Christine. People know that being a leader involves having and controlling an agenda. They became frustrated when she did not do that.

But the commitment to stay and work through what went on in the group meant that people did not just give the group up as a bad job, as we often do in the ordinary world when things are not going as we 'know' they should. The group leader, Christine, said that she suspected people were frustrated with her, making meaningful sense of what a number of people were experiencing. By this attribution of a meaning to the feelings of the group, and the implication that there were alternative possibilities, people were able to see something of what they were projecting, something of what alternatives there were for the group, and something of who the leader was in a different way.

The most troublesome projections tend to be those recognized by object-relations theory as the image of the threatening or the frustrating other, to which we have well-practised responses.

In the group of chapter 6 Ms Emma H's promising/frustrating projections were called into play by her meeting with Ian. As an unknown person he offered echoes of the attention she longed for, and at first he seemed to hold out the promise of his interest in her. Emma was excited and enlivened by this. But he proved disappointing, and Emma was thrown back into the reverse side of her response: 'I'll just go through the polite formalities, but really I've withdrawn.' For Emma, and for all of us taken up in such a projection, the response seems the only one possible, and typically too, we are unaware of some aspects of it. For instance we might be unaware of the powerful effect of pushing the other away, or that we had expected the other to do something specific.

The intervention of Christine allowed Emma to see that something of this response was her own. Indeed it was just the response she always made when people failed to live up to expectations that they had once excited. It became, in that realization, difficult simply to disown her share in the responsibility for what happened. By owning it she could perhaps move beyond it and see something of the person Ian, rather than just the usual 'disappointing man' in yet another manifestation.

Presumably the origin of this kind of projection is in the defensiveness against what were seen as parental attitudes of being attractive and promising, but then disappointing. In Emma's case she had presumably decided that in her family, to make any kind of fuss made things much worse, and that she was unlikely to get the recognition she wanted.

So in discovering that she felt despairing and resentful rather than simply being patient as she thought, and by saying some of the unsayable things associated with these projections to the person at whom they were directed, a step was made towards withdrawing some of them. The implicit theory of how to act which might have been appropriate for a father who occasionally took an interest in his daughter, but who then had more important things to do, may not be quite appropriate for a man in the group.

The possibility of play

The atmosphere of safety plus challenge is an analogue of play. Play is relatively safe. As defined by adults at least, it is 'not serious'. By somewhat reducing the costs of making mistakes, the possibility arises of being able to make mistakes and thereby learn. If we do learn from mistakes, the environments we provide for learning should be spaces in which it is possible to make them. Though play is in a way 'not serious', it is also where the most serious things of life are experimented with. It is not so much that play is by definition safe. It can be risky, unpredictable, engaging, exciting. Once one has entered through Goffman's (1961) 'semi-permeable membrane' of a face-to-face interaction, one either takes one's life and existence from the mutually understood rules, a step which may have unpredictable consequences, or one does what one can to control the interaction, or else simply goes through the motions, until one can leave.

By providing a space which is not safe, but somewhat safer than the way the ordinary world is perceived, a group allows people the possibility of a decrease in the need to control their interactions rigidly, and the possibility to see what happens if they do not just leave.

9

Emotions and cultural experience

In this final chapter my aim is to draw the threads together. I return to the first person voice of chapter 1 to discuss why emotions are involved both in our disturbances and in our possibilities of change, and to explore the metaphor of therapy as play. Individual therapy and groups are not about anybody doing anything to anyone. They are not a means to the end of changing that person because we know best what should be. It is more like play, in which although people do all sorts of things, the purpose of play is simply itself.

Emotions

In some kinds of emotional state, such as excitement or sadness, a person may experience a wave of that emotion, and then perhaps experience something else, maybe experience being with another person who is present. Other kinds of emotion are longer lasting, they wipe out all possibility of taking part in anything except the narrowly focused subject which they have taken up. Often their ruminations lay waste any possibility of experiencing the ordinary world. It is to these latter kinds of emotion that therapists most often attend: to envy, to pride, to vengefulness, to guilt, to jealousy, to anxiety.

It is not accidental that this list reminds one of lists of deadly sins. Sin as described by Kierkegaard (1849) is precisely a disrelation with oneself, and a disrelation with others. These matters are seen as illnesses by psychiatrists, but they might more appropriately be seen as matters of ethics, as has been argued in this book. The insight of therapy is that these disrelations are not abolished by saying to oneself or others 'don't be envious', 'don't be jealous', 'don't be embittered'.

Anxiety

As I approached finishing this book I found myself being swept along on a tide of just such an emotion: anxiety. The deadline approached. I had taken on far too much, and there was not time to do it all, to fulfil my commitments and obligations. I found myself preoccupied, and irritable with other people, waking up at five in the morning, not to write and hence complete the writing, but to lie awake ruminating.

All these feelings had a kind of compulsiveness about them, a lack of space. I felt driven. I couldn't help being preoccupied. Or so I felt. Not with activities relevant to the things I worried about, for example getting the book finished. One person complained (rightly) to me for being withdrawn and grumpy.

Two features of this are noticeable. One is the sense of lack of space. It is as if the world turns from having room for choice, for possibility, for being productive or creative, to having no room in it to move except to be propelled down a narrow windowless corridor. My behaviour seemed to consist of doing things both to myself, that is remonstrating with myself, and to others, like being irritable and withdrawn. Any space to be, to allow, even to do the things I wanted to do, like finish writing the book, had vanished.

The second noticeable thing is that my concerns were what psychoanalysts call narcissistic. They didn't really have to do with writing the book, or being with the people I was with. They had to do with me, and my reflection of myself to myself in mirror of egotistical concerns. They had to do with whether I had time to make the book as good as I wanted to in my imagination, or worse still, whether I could.

Instead of doing what I was doing, I was compulsively and irritably worrying.

Expectation of mutuality

Many of the more distressing emotions to which we are subject arise when there is a mismatch between our plans or aspirations, and the actuality of the world. Most intensely, they occur when plans and aspirations have, as we thought, been mutual in some way, involving another or others. So the most common disaster that leads people to emotional crises or breakdowns is a loss of some sort, the breakup or loss of a relationship, loss of a job, failure of some longed-for expectation, an unfavourable re-evaluation of someone who has been close. Typically in such events, a sense of mutuality is shattered. A husband might think, 'If I do well in my career, then she will love me.' Or a mother may think, 'If I make sure my son has the best of everything then he will be happy and a credit to me.' I had been thinking, 'I've been working hard on this book so people should make allowances.' But these trustful expectations are shattered when the man's wife becomes discontented, when the mother's son gets into trouble with the police, when I'm told I should stop being so irritable.

It is an assumed mutual arrangement that is shattered, and the sense of the shatterment reverberates as Katz (1980) says in a wavelike fashion, so that the person may feel now lost, now longing, now regretful, now sad, now angry, now envious, now embittered, now vengeful, now anxious and apprehensive that yet further reverses will occur. These dysphoric emotions, and their accompanying obsessive ruminations, trying to fit the world back into order, can take over a person's life. As Foulds (1965) points out they disrupt the person's sense of selfhood.

Since so often the adversity is an apparent failure of mutuality, the emotion might be the occasion for an understanding that one had perhaps been projecting inappropriate expectations on to the other: that a husband had been assuming he would be loved if he got on with his career, and in so doing entirely neglect the things that his wife was saying or feeling. A mother in providing all the things she thinks are necessary in child-rearing might neglect the fact that her son feels unhappy. I had been neglecting the fact that it is because of my own choices that I take on too much and therefore feel pressured by others.

The crisis is an opportunity to learn something about one's own relating, and about the nature of the other, just as in psychotherapy there is the opportunity in the surprise of an interpretation or a dramatization, to learn something about oneself and the other.

However, sometimes the emotion is too overwhelming. Instead of changing or learning anything, we increase our sense of self-importance, hanging more tenaciously than ever on to what we believe: we become defensive. We might decide to restrict our goals or narrow our plans. 'I'll do without any close relationship, I think I'd be happier really.' Or we project the problem on to others, and become vengeful, sulky, embittered. 'I did my very best but it still didn't make any difference.'

It is under circumstances such as these, where the space of any kind of flexible or negotiated participation in the world has narrowed, that a person is in distress. Such a person may seek therapy, and may have no sense that what is broken was a sense of mutuality with others and with society. Simply an area of meaning has evaporated.

The rules which constitute a person's life may seem so obvious to her or him as not even to be worth formulating. Perhaps for that very reason the person may be unaware of them, or their pervasiveness, just as one might imagine that a goldfish would be unaware of the water in which it swims round and round.

It seems impossible that some another person who we think we know well may have been following rules that we assumed were similar, but which are quite different.

Laing *et al.* (1966) quote the case of a couple who on their honeymoon went to have a drink in the bar of their hotel. The newly married wife struck up conversation with another couple sitting there. The new husband became sulky, taciturn, and refused to join in. Afterwards they had a serious row, the first of their marriage. Eight years later in therapy they could laugh about it. She had wanted to try out her new social role as 'married person' by having a conversation with another married couple. He had felt that on this occasion, above all others, they could just be together alone, and for her to want to talk to anyone else could mean only that she found him inadequate. Both assumed a mutuality, which indeed they had established over a wide area of their lives. But both also assumed that their idiosyncratic rules were shared completely by the other.

Defence against hurt

When some such sense of mutual knowledge is shared and acted on by the other, there is a sense of gratitude, of trust, and of feeling recognized. But when it is contradicted there is a sense of bewilderment and betrayal. As for this couple, the other person comes to appear as being deliberately hurtful.

In response to such hurts a person may construct quite long-term solutions or defences. And in so far as the solution brings in its train consequences which are as bad as the problem, these solutions tend to be called neurotic. So for instance if like Ms Cindy S a person builds herself a small island of safety, she might find that this is so restricting that practically anything else she might want is unreachable, and she consumes her life in envy. A person like Mr Hal D might find himself, after a disappointment, in despair. Because he is not engaged in his daily actions, he finds life futile and empty. A person like Ms Emma H might feel discontented and hopeless without understanding how this has to do with another not having fulfilled expectations which were not even made explicit between them. I was being preoccupied and anxious without acknowledging how withdrawn and rejecting I was being to others.

Freud's emphasis on the unconscious becoming conscious can be translated into questions of honesty, and the explicitness of what is assumed to be mutual. We usually do not attend to the rules by which we live, sometimes we are quite unaware of them, but at the same time expect others to live by the same rules.

In the more public life of a community, rules are shared. Many of the pronouncements of the ancient law-givers, once perhaps heard as authoritative voices, are written down and known to all members of a society: 'Honour thy father and mother'; 'Thou shalt not kill'. At this level there is seldom doubt as to what is the right or appropriate thing to do in a culture. People who disobey such rules are assumed to transgress knowingly. In certain cases they are called criminals.

But more personal rules, for example 'Now we are married we

will be able to have friendships with other married couples', may not even be known to the other. Yet it is rules of this kind which are most precious, and which pervade our most intimate relationships. For the most part people seek therapy because things have gone wrong with these intimate arrangements of mutuality.

Rules one learns in one's family often are idiosyncratic, rules of what one needs to do to be loved or respected, or to avoid censure. It is in this sense that relationships in the adult world can be thought of as being built on the foundations of one's earliest relationships. It is in this sense that transference means the attempt to engage the other in structures of these foundational rules. But though appropriate to one's early family, they may no longer be appropriate. But, because they are so pervasive, we can be unaware of them.

The interpretation or the dramatization brings them to light. The transference is a kind of playground in which the therapist both is and is not the mother or father of one's earliest relating. And the dramas that take place in groups, in the theatre and in one's life both are and are not the explorations of the consequences of these rules which appear, as the ancient Greeks would say, as one's destiny.

In so far as one is consumed with the pain, bitterness, anxiety or despair of a discrepancy between what we have assumed and what has turned out in the world of our intimates, then we find there is no space. There is only the compulsiveness of incessant rumination, and the drivenness of actions, the trying to put the world back into shape.

But in so far as the drama of one's life can be seen as a kind of play, then one can take part in it, and a space to be opens up.

Creativity and selfhood

The person who coined the metaphors of space and linked them to the possibilities of playing was Winnicott (1971, 1979). Playing according to him is primary, and is perhaps the major healing process. Psychotherapy is a specialized form of playing invented in the twentieth century. 'Psychotherapy', writes Winnicott (1971),

> has to do with two people playing together. The corollary of this is that where playing is not possible then the work done by the therapist is directed towards bringing the patient from

a state of not being able to play into a state of being able to play. (p. 44)

In the light of this we can see either Freud's injunction to free-associate, or Moreno's explorations in psychodrama just as Winnicott says, as forms of playing. Free-associating is to let oneself fall into the involuntary play of images, to let these images and language play in the presence of the other person. The transference is not simply the irritating intrusion of fantasies of past figures projected on to the person of the therapist. It is the domain of playing where I find myself acting towards the therapist as if she or he were my mother or my father. The forms of dramatization, from the playing of children with human figures, for example as introduced into therapy by Klein (1955) to the psychodrama of Moreno (1940), to the interactions of groups, are even more obviously playful. They take place in worlds of metaphor and symbol. Such worlds are typical of the world of culture: it is founded on a kind of (perfectly proper) illusion, where what is real for us comes into being.

Winnicott links these matters on the one hand to what he calls transitional phenomena and on the other to a person's emergence into culture, into creativity, and into an experience of selfhood.

Transitional phenomena

Transitional phenomena can be observed in quite young children. They typically occur where children discover what Winnicott calls a 'transitional object'. The object may be a thumb to suck, perhaps a toy or blanket or some piece of material to carry round. Such a transitional object has an apparently magical effect for the child. For instance with the object she or he can be soothed and fall to sleep when it is time to do so. Without it the child can be distraught.

Transitional objects, and/or activities of this kind, says Winnicott, are the first young shoots of human culture, pushing through the soil of human development.

To start with, the good-enough mother and her baby are essentially one. The baby seems to have desires, for instance for the breast. Winnicott (1971) says that the baby develops a 'subjective' phenomenon, perhaps creates a kind of image of the breast, and to start with, magically, 'the mother places the actual breast just where the baby is ready to create, and at the right moment' (p. 13). But this will not go on for ever. The illusion is to be broken in the process of weaning. In this disillusion, if all goes well, the baby who at first was merged completely with its mother, starts to experience her as separate, not simply as an extension of its own subjectivity or its internal world.

It is the space, or rather the potential space in between the child and the mother, which becomes the space where play occurs. To start with it may be the transitional object, the blanket or whatever, which comes to occupy this space. It is, as Winnicott says, the child's first 'not me' possession. It is not a part of the internal world, not a hallucination or image. Nor is it an external object. It is in between. Though it may represent the mother or her comfortingness, it is not her. The object, if it is an object (it might be a ritual or some activity instead) is not exactly created by the child. Nor is it exactly discovered in the outside world. It is somewhere in between. It is transitional, at the border.

The eventual fate of the object is that it is gradually de-cathected. It is not lost or mourned but gradually sinks into limbo as its meaning vanishes, and is replaced by the more diffuse and various activities of play and of cultural activity. It becomes, as Winnicott says, 'spread out over the whole intermediate territory between "inner psychic reality" and "the external world as perceived by two persons in common", that is to say the whole cultural field' (p. 6). It becomes the person's participation in the order of the symbolic, including the order of language.

Creativity

Winnicott shows that entry into the symbolic order can become terribly disrupted. The usual subjective sense of the disruption is a sense that something somehow is deeply and irremediably wrong. What is wrong can be seen in terms of a person's sense of a lack of meaning, an absence of a sense of creativity in her or his life.

It is this creative sense, says Winnicott, which

> more than anything else makes the individual feel that life is worth living. Contrasted with this is a relationship to external reality which is one of compliance. . . . Compliance carries with it a sense of futility for the individual and is associated with the

idea that nothing matters, and that life is not worth living. In a tantalizing way many individuals have experienced just enough of creative living to recognise that they are living uncreatively, as if caught up in the creativity of someone else, or of a machine. (p. 76)

Play is quite the opposite of compliance. Playing is what one does for its own sake, not for any particular end, and not because someone else might want one to, even when what is done is supposedly 'for one's own good'. It is therapeutic in itself. It occurs where some other who is known from experience to be trustworthy will take part.

Negotiation and recognition

Two elements seem essential: one is the sense of negotiability, though this is perhaps not a good word. It is the sense that what one might do has an effect, contributes, is potent. It is the sense in which in a good relationship the rules of what can occur are continually undergoing evolution. As in children's play suggestions can be made, explicitly or implicitly, and they may or may not be taken up and incorporated. But this contrasts with the sense of stubbornness which occurs when someone feels she or he is being forced to do something in a way which is non-negotiable.

The other and related element is that what a person gives forth in play needs to be recognized by the other. Of course not everything is recognized in quite the way anticipated – there may be an element of challenge. The other may select, respond to some things, not others. But play depends on the other witnessing and understanding the meaning of what is given forth, reflecting it back, changing it somewhat, keeping it in play. The elements of negotiation and recognition are, of course, similar to the conditions for individual therapy and groups: containment and interpretation, safety and challenge.

These paired elements contribute fundamentally to creating a world of experiencing. With the witness and participation of the other, in the activities of play, the person can establish a meaningful sense of self. Without negotiation and recognition, selfhood seems impossible.

The contrast with 'being done to'

But playing is not something one person does to or for another. Nor does the experience take place, at least to start with, in an inner world, or an outer world. It occurs in a third area, in between. It is in the light of the reflections of play that the person may discover her or himself.

Bateson tells an anecdote about play. A psychiatrist and a schizophrenic patient were playing golf together. To their surprise they both became engrossed in the game, lost themselves in it, or should one say found themselves? As the last ball was putted in, the psychiatrist suddenly 'realized what had been happening', that this sick, refractory, schizophrenic patient had been behaving normally. In an impulse of good intention he said, 'Would you like another round?' The schizophrenic patient said nothing, and walked away. No doubt he had gathered that playing golf had stopped, and that he was now about to be humoured, done good to.

In Winnicott's view exploitation of the area of transitional phenomena, of play, especially in a child's early years whether by intrusions, or the forcing of compliant behaviour, or by deprivations, leaves the person with a clutter of 'persecutory elements [in his inner world] which he has no means of ridding himself' (p. 121).

This contrast between play and compliance may throw light on that difficult problem, the nature of love. As Laing (1967) puts it,

> Love and violence, properly speaking, are polar opposites. Love lets the other be, but with affection and concern. Violence attempts to constrain the other's freedom, to force him to act in the way we desire, but with ultimate lack of concern. (p. 50)

Winnicott links the experience of an intrusion or violation of this area of creativity to what he calls the development of a 'false self'. It is a kind of caretaker who will stand in for oneself in the world, acting and performing as a self might act, and perhaps even being essentially indistinguishable by others from an actual self, but who is really a protective front. People committed to hiding behind a false self are often in severe distress, feeling that either they have lost their 'true self' or that they await the conditions when the true self will be able to emerge.

The image of 'false self', protective against dangerous pressures, is evocative and recognizable to many as a portrait of their alienated experience. However, it has a somewhat unfortunate quality. A false self can be a routine, a script, a pattern, a role, or even a bundle of roles. It is a mistake, though, to suppose that there is a corresponding true self, equally reified and fixed as a role or pattern of some kind although not defensive or compliant. A trend of ego-psychology has fostered the notion that the goal of therapy is to discover what kind of 'me' or what kind of 'thing' this true self really is. To become immersed in this question is again to lose the sense of play. In playing, on the contrary, the 'thingness' on which egoism seems to thrive, is lost, and a self, not fixed but participating, is found.

The subversion of the ego

The French psychoanalyst Lacan (1966) has done his best to undermine this quest for the discovery of a whole, true self. The quest for a rediscovery of wholeness is a regressive fantasy, a longing for the idea that once we felt whole, in that merger of self and mother, of which the stories of the fall from Paradise are mythic echoes, he says. The awful fact is that we have fallen, and that the paradisiac merger is no longer possible.

Lacan writes that the task of therapy is to allow the subject to enter into the order of the symbolic, the order of language, that is to say of culture. One goes to a therapist, as ancients went to the oracle. But in visiting the oracle/therapist one may not understand that answers to the questions like 'How am I to be happy?' will not be forthcoming. The oracle 'neither speaks out nor conceals, but gives a sign' (Heraclitus in Kirk and Raven (eds), 1957).

The name of the father

Our entry into culture and into the symbolic takes place not as a matter of biological development, but precisely out of the social arrangements whereby as children we see, or feel, or sense, that the paradisiac union with our mother is lost. Or were things ever all right, and is even that longing for a lost unity just an idealized, split-off image which will haunt us, and direct our earthly quest?

Lacan sees the father, or perhaps at least the symbolic presence of the father, the name of the father, as that which prohibits this incestuous longing. Though it may be clear biologically who our mother is, it is by the force of law, the father's law, that we know our father and are given a name. In our society it is our father's name that we are given.

In the Oedipal realization that we are not just one with our mother, our entry into the world of the symbolic begins. For our longing to have our mother all to ourself, in some sort of biological merger, is unfulfillable. We seek its partial fulfilments in lovers who never quite satisfy, in aims that when achieved seem to turn to ashes in our mouths. Our desire, as Lacan intimates, is caught up on a long chain of displacements of which we are unaware, but which link back inevitably to that first and irretrievable relationship.

We live in the adult world with no possibility of wholeness. Like our political images of some future Utopia, it is a fantasy. Our longings and desires in every domain of life, are proof of that sense of lack. If that were not enough, each renewal of a desire reminds us that the last one has indeed not satisfied us. We are creatures seemingly in permanent search for something.

Except that even our desire is not really ours. It is as Lacan says the desire of the Other. Ambiguously it is both our own desire, and the desire that we shall be the one who the Other loves and wants.

But of course this other too may be a kind of reflection of our own needs, just as we take ourselves to be what we imagine others think of us. So we find ourselves living in a world of reflections, the order as Lacan says of the 'imaginary', of images.

In Lacan's writings, or more correctly in the translations of his writings, 'Other' is spelled sometimes with a large 'O', sometimes with a small 'o'. The Other is that Other who disturbs our comfortable sense of being in control of things, is the Other of surprises, of the unpredictable, ultimately the uncontrollable, the separate. But as in Mead's theory of the self, and in object-relations theory we try to make sure this other stays predictable, in roles, in arrangements, in deals. In so far as we succeed in doing so we succeed however in producing only an other with a small 'o', a domesticated other, who will fit in with our imagination, conform to our efforts to control the relationship. But in doing so, the Other as 'different' necessarily eludes us. We are faced merely with a reflection of an image, and hence live in the order of the imaginary.

It is by being Other, a third presence disturbing the comfortable arrangement of mother and child, that the father, or at least the name of the father, institutes the person's entry into language.

By being Other, by refusing to be simply domesticated into the ordinary interpersonal manoeuvres of the client the therapist too declines the invitation simply to be a reflection in the eyes of the client, simply an imaginary other.

For Lacan, and for a group of feminists of his school (see for example Mitchell and Rose, 1982; Gallop, 1982) it has not escaped attention that the entry into culture, and the unwillingness to make that entry, is signalled by the male 'name of the father' as we are inducted into the father's family. Any culture we do enter is patriarchal; any unwillingness to enter it is labelled by males 'neurotic'. In the twentieth century, as for the early Greeks, many of the voices of cultural injunctions and prohibitions in our heads tend to be male.

An alienated sense of being

Lacan's project is in part to show that life is not the quest to fulfil some biological function in human life, but rather that we take our experience from the culture that we are born into. There is no 'true self' to discover, as one might discover an oak tree after leaving an acorn undisturbed for a period of time.

But by finding our being in culture, aspects of our existence will necessarily be alien. The slips of the tongue, the dreams, the neuroses, are all reminders that no one of us is a single agent, able to get life fully under control, and buttoned up. Freud's discovery of the unconscious is the discovery that what we take ourselves to be, is to some large extent not under control, it is Other.

This is not some defect to be remedied by sufficient therapy, so that we shall find ourselves whole again. Rather it is the radical split at the centre of our being. As Mitchell (1982) puts it, Lacan's

> subject is not an entity with an identity, but a being created in the fissure of a radical split. The identity that seems to be that of the subject is in fact a mirage arising when the subject forms an image of itself by identifying with others' perceptions of it. (p. 5)

Putting this another way, it is a silly conceit to think that we speak

147

language, control it, communicate to pre-existing others in the world by using it. Rather language speaks us.

Our sex roles which are the first and most obvious means by which we are all defined (is it a girl or a boy?), remind us not of the possibility of wholeness, or of having things under control, but of incompleteness, and of not having the most important matters under control at all. The Other who we hope to meet in sexual relationships is radically uncontrollable. To try to control a human situation, for instance, to try and ensure that love is predictable, perhaps by making someone a slave who can only accede to our demand, would be precisely and completely to have killed any possibility of love.

We try to demand 'love'. Indeed the demand for love is perhaps our most earnest and incessant wish, which emerges in therapy as elsewhere. But in so far as we try to tame the other, and manoeuvre her or him into loving us, we have lost our own being.

Matters like love, or play, are wayward. They are not to be subdued by a self who is in control. But the perturbations brought on by the Other, the out-of-control excitements and the intrusive terrors, are just as much self, as anything else about us.

Object-relations theorists with their talk of splitting of some pre-existing self, which might be regained, have diluted some of Freud's discoveries. Therapy is not just the healing of these splits. Building a sense of agency is fundamental, and often people's lives founder on not being able to achieve things they set out to do. Some of these aims are helped by practical politics, and others by therapy. But the involuntary, the unconscious, the Other, are parts of life too. These are parts of our lives, although they are not easily identifiable with a single centre, a 'me' in control of things. They emerge from the community of which an 'I' is only part. We gain our experience by participating. 'Me' may not like that, but it is part of 'I'. And the world is partly a world of playing. It is symbolic.

Two matters remain however which are the themes of this book, both raised by Lacan's attacks on the orthodox worlds of institutionalized psychoanalysis. First, what is the nature of this society into which we are born, and from which we take our being? Second, what is the experience of selfhood in relation to others, towards which therapy points, even granted that it can neither be any kind of fixed, reified 'thing', not a return to some imagined, undivided, and untroubled state?

The possibility of a non-patriarchal society

Sexuality is one of our most forceful reminders of the fragmentariness of our selfhood. What seems even worse is that sexuality has become transformed into various kinds of exploitation and derogation in the cause of trying to subdue the Other. Dinnerstein (1976) concludes that however we may have created the inequities and power structures between women and men, it seems likely that we maintain them by ensuring that women have the virtual monopoly of child-rearing.

What this means is that both women and men grow up from a basis in which, as stressed by Winnicott, their first love was a woman. If then there is anything in the possibility that our relating is founded on the prototypes of these earliest patterns of intimate relationship, this fact is likely to have a profound effect.

Dinnerstein argues that it has the effect which indeed we see in our society. Growing up involves a disappointment: one cannot have one's first love, one's mother, to oneself. Perhaps indeed one never did have. It is a disappointment which according both to object-relations theory and to Lacan, we never properly get over. It leaves us with that sense of unsatisfiable lack which is the source of our desire.

It also produces a splitting. Unable to contain the idea that the person whom we loved is the same person who disappointed us, we split the two, and create two images: an idealized image of the perfect mother, whom we then proceed to seek for, and reinstantiate in other relationships with friends and lovers, and an equivalent image of the bad frustrating mother whom we defend ourselves against.

One can notice, as Dinnerstein points out, that in a society where women bring up children, it is principally women who are the recipients of these projections.

As far as men are concerned women are to be adored, sought after, idealized, seen as the source of love and affection, to be placated, and wooed; and they are despised, laughed at in sexist jokes, not taken seriously, systematically deprived of power and influence. For Dinnerstein this effect is not a result of biology, not a result of men being on average physically stronger and therefore able to be more exploitative, not an accident of history. It occurs precisely because women are the objects both of the desire and of the disappointment of men.

Women too are brought up by mothers. But they discover that they also are women, and many of them perhaps more uneasily transfer their sexual attentions to men. This is helped perhaps by a less problematic, often courtly, interest of their father or some equivalent male figure.

Though women very often find men 'disappointing', they can also themselves maintain an even more archaic sense, equivalent to that of men, that women are disappointing too, are also alternately adorable and despicable. But in contrast with men, for women these images rebound on the self as well.

For object-relations theorists, such as Dinnerstein, the goal of therapy is to reintegrate this split: idealized and despised, good and bad. To come to see mother as perhaps not perfect, but actually all right. In the same way, therapy although a disappointment in that the self is not magically reborn, comes to seem quite good and the therapist, though with some unsatisfactory features, is worth having known.

If there is truth in her analysis, then Dinnerstein's conclusion also follows: the only fundamental way we might hope to instantiate a society with much chance of being non-sexist is that fathers and mothers take equal share in child-rearing, so that both become the targets of intense love, and intense disappointment. There are fierce resistances against it, of course, both from current women and current men. Such a society, moreover, might lead to an even more complete misanthropy/misogyny, rather than the more simple currents of misogyny practised now. But there is also the hope that under these circumstances, projections of adoration and scorn, since they would be made to both sexes, might be more easily seen through.

Self experience

Despite Lacan's rejection of the idea of any kind of integrated self, there remains the need to talk of the difference between being troubled in the sense of taken over by compulsions or avoidances, and being able to play, to take part in life.

Lacan is right in that such a reborn self is not a thing, a new social 'me' to be seen in a more benign mirror than the previous one. Nevertheless people do talk of feeling different as a result of therapy. The empirical evidence also indicates that people are different.

It seems that as a result of individual therapy or groups, people do feel more themselves, more able to cope, more autonomous, more able to make choices, more able to take responsibility for themselves. And as the empirical research indicates, symptoms which so often were fears, embarrassments, excuses, somatizations, sulks, lies, manoeuvres, bargaining counters, are replaced with a more direct participation. The language of symptoms gives way to a more direct kind of speaking with each other.

But all this, though not negligible by any means, still leaves something elusively unsaid.

Khan (1972) calls this elusive sense 'self experience'. Its coming marks a turning-point in therapy, after which the person can feel situated in the world, in her or his body (cf. Merleau-Ponty, 1960), and able to play. Khan says the difficulty is that whereas in writing about therapy, it is possible to describe an interpretation of a particular defence, when one comes to describe a 'self experience' it can sound quite banal. It is not so much to do with having made these or those interpretations, but of having taken part in a certain kind of being-with-that-person.

What gets left out of most accounts of therapy, perhaps because it sounds, as Khan supposes, too banal, or perhaps because it is another of those matters which cannot be spoken about directly, is that something important goes on, not for the therapist, not for the client, but between them. Something that sometimes pivots around a single moment or incident, but which makes a difference to the client, just simply in being able to experience . . .

. . . Experience what? Not self exactly. That sounds too fixed, too *self*-centred. It is nothing much to do with self really, but more like losing self. It is not the other, with small or big 'o'. Perhaps more as Winnicott says, it is something in between. Perhaps it is just a moment of being present, but a moment witnessed and recognized. It has nothing to do with symptoms, or the therapist being clever, but it involves both in a taking part. It is a moment not to be captured or possessed, but one that can make a difference in always being able to recreate that sense again. It needs in the first instance to be created in the play of discourse with another but then in a certain way it becomes one's own.

What is born in therapy is not a kind of reconditioned 'me'. 'Me', after all, is not above being something of a public relations officer. What is reborn is 'I' who can be in relation to 'you', taking part in what is going on.

The end of psychotherapy

What is the end, the goal towards which therapy tends, which therapy seeks for? In the directive therapies the client comes to be relieved of her or his symptoms, is helped with what she or he wants to do but cannot. This does not remove the interplay of personal negotiations in the relationship between client and therapist, or the question of whether the answers found were the ones the client wanted. In non-directive and interpretive therapy, no suggestions about what to do are made: 'Just come and say what occurs to you', or in a group 'Just come and take part in what goes on.' The client on the one hand can scarcely avoid doing that, on the other hand finds that she or he cannot do it.

The injunction is to play, to take part in what is going on. The malady is precisely that the client, all of us, for some or much of the time cannot or do not take part in what is going on. We want to hang on to some fixed 'me' rather than being 'I' with 'you'.

So deep is the sense that the self as a 'me' is an ultimate truth, that we do not realize either the pervasiveness or the implications of this assumption. As Heidegger (1954) has laboured to show, this kind of assumption cuts us off from Being, and from experience.

I asked a man I met who had become a Buddhist what difference becoming a Buddhist had made to him. He said, 'The difference is that now when I'm making lasagne, what I'm doing is making lasagne.' I took it that he meant he was not worrying about whether it was going to turn out all right, whether the people he was making it for would enjoy it and think he was a good cook, what he might be doing later, what he ought to be doing now.

Part of Zen Buddhist discipline is to study koans (see for example Miura and Sasaki, 1965). Koans may seem paradoxical, but their purpose is to reach the experience of a more enlightened understanding. Like life, koans can't be 'solved' logically, worked out in advance to see what is to be done. Perhaps better than regarding them as paradoxes, they might be regarded as sayings which are simple and direct, but from an enlightened way of being, different from that of 'me'. People meditate on these koans until they penetrate their inner meaning. A Zen master, perhaps a bit like a psychotherapist, will listen to a Zen student's response to a koan, and be able to tell whether it proceeds from a state of being within its meaning, or from something second-hand, or from a desire to get it right, or to show off, or from an intellectualization.

A famous koan of Hakuin Zenji (Miura and Sasaki, 1965, p. 44) is 'Listen to the sound of the Single Hand!', often transformed in the west to 'What is the sound of one hand clapping?' It would be possible to give an answer, but to do so would be to suggest there was an answer, a solution to the puzzle which one could take away. But that would be precisely not the answer. It would not be taking part in the play of meditation, and the engagement in that. It would merely be a result, like finding out the result of a problem in arithmetic.

Just as in ethics, there is not always a point in saying, 'Don't do that', so in therapy if a therapist were to say 'The answer is that you should go out more', or 'You should get on with your life rather than regretting what is past and feeling embittered about it', this would be unlikely to do much good. It would be an answer. It might even be the correct answer. But it would not help. In these matters the issue is not just truth, but the person's relation to that truth: whether she or he appropriates it.

People come to therapy because they can't get on with living. Then in therapy or in a group they find that they can't just take part in what is going on, for its own sake, even though that's all there is. The 'answer', an answer, any answer, would turn out to be empty, useless, to be discarded as soon as heard, as not the answer. Not that one. There must be more.

Like Buddhists, some psychotherapists insist that all that is going on in therapy is what is going on. Like a koan, the relationship of therapy is simply itself. An end in itself, not something with some other end. It is simply a matter of being present, participating in what one is doing, although it often takes a long time to reach this, working through projections, resistances and transferences. But in the end, participating in the relationship is what there is. The doing of therapy is not a means to an end of

153

getting better (though one does get better). It is the end in itself. The taking part in it is the 'I' that I am seeking.

But there must be more.

Taking part

The trouble is that, as Lacan intimates, we always feel there must be more. We are founded in lack, and that prevents us from taking part in what we are doing. We don't accept that radically, we are part. We want it all, the whole, to be whole. And that becomes more important than to be doing what we are doing.

To be able to fix, to capture the answer, would of course be to kill off play. One can see it when an adult interferes to tell a child, 'You shouldn't do it like this, but like that.' The adult may be right, but play has been stopped. Something else has become more important. What the child was not doing became more important than what it was doing. And if one is not careful the joy may drain out of it.

It is not that play is all there is. The productive order of work in which we have definite ends in mind is fundamental to human beings as well. But to be unable ever to take part in what one is doing (including work), to be for ever doing things for some other reason, which of course always postpones the doing of what we would actually like to be doing, is the lack of the sense of creativity that Winnicott (1971) wrote about.

Matters which are ends in themselves may be only part of a life in which other parts are means towards ends, our own or those seemingly imposed by other people. But without that part, we seem devoid of experiencing who we are at all.

Not that there are no rules, not that life could be without prohibitions. Rules enable rather than prevent play. Just as the rules of formation of a sonnet, fourteen lines with accents thus and thus, have allowed for some the creativity of poetry. A mutual understanding of the rules of society, primarily in language, allows us to play together, to be separate individuals but in community.

We are deprived of the primal togetherness of being at one with nature like the animals, or of the historical togetherness with the mother of our earliest days. We have become separate, and feel that lack keenly. The compensation is human culture and relating to those whom we are with.

Benne, K.D. (1964) 'History of the T-group in the laboratory setting', in Bradford, L.P., Benne, K.D. and Gibb, J.R. (eds) *T-group Theory and Laboratory Method: Innovation in Re-education*, New York, Wiley. *94*

Bergin, A.E. (1971) 'The evaluation of therapeutic outcomes', in Bergin, A.E. and Garfield, S.L. (eds) *Handbook of Psychotherapy and Behavior Change: an Empirical Analysis*, New York, Wiley. *75, 111*

Bhaskar, R. (1975) *A Realist Theory of Science*, Brighton, Harvester. *85*

Brown, G.W. and Harris, T. (1978) *Social Origins of Depression*, London, Tavistock. *24–5*

Buber, M. (1923) *I and Thou*, trans. R.G. Smith, Edinburgh, Clark. *71*

Congreve, W. (1700) *The Way of the World*, London, Dent. *15*

Cooley, C. (1902) *Human Nature and the Social Order*, New York, Scribner. *20*

Descartes, R. (1637) *Discourse on Method*, trans. F.E. Sutcliffe, Harmondsworth, Penguin. *36*

Dinnerstein, D. (1976) *The Rocking of the Cradle and the Ruling of the World*, London, Souvenir Press. *149–50*

Edgley, R. (1981) Lectures on the philosophy of science, University of Sussex. *67*

Eysenck, H.J. (1952) 'The effects of psychotherapy: an evaluation', *Journal of Consulting Psychology*, 16, 319–24. *75*

Eysenck, H.J. (ed.) (1960) *Behaviour Therapy and the Neuroses*, Oxford, Pergamon. *75–6*

Fairbairn, W.R.D. (1952) *Psychoanalytic Studies of the Personality*, London, Routledge & Kegan Paul. *22–3*

Foulds, G.A. (1965) *Personality and Personal Illness*, London, Tavistock. *34*

Foulds, G.A. (1976) *The Hierarchical Nature of Personal Illness*, London, Academic Press. *34, 137*

Freud, S. (1895) in Breuer, J. and Freud, S. *Studies on Hysteria*, trans. A. and J. Strachey, Pelican Freud Library, vol. 3, Harmondsworth, Pelican. *8*

Freud, S. (1901) *The Psychopathology of Everyday Life*, trans. A. Tyson, Pelican Freud Library, vol. 5, Harmondsworth, Pelican. *63, 80*

Freud, S. (1905) *Case Histories, 1: Dora and Little Hans*, trans. A. and J. Strachey, Pelican Freud Library, vol. 8, Harmondsworth, Pelican. *63*

Freud, S. (1916–17) *Introductory Lectures on Psychoanalysis*, trans. J. Strachey, Pelican Freud Library, vol. 1, Harmondsworth, Pelican. *17*

Freud, S. (1923) *The Ego and the Id*, trans. J. Riviere, New York, Norton. *22*

Gallop, J. (1982) *Feminism and Psychoanalysis: the Daughter's Seduction*, London, Macmillan. *147*

Garfield, S.L. and Bergin, A.E. (eds) (1978) *Handbook of Psychotherapy and Behaviour Change: an Empirical Analysis*, 2nd edn, New York, Wiley. *80*

Gardiner, M. (ed.) (1972) *The Wolf-man and Sigmund Freud*, Harmondsworth, Pelican. *80*

Goffman, E. (1961) *Encounters: Two Studies in the Sociology of Interaction*, Indianapolis, Bobbs-Merrill. *13–19, 63, 121, 134*

Green, H. (1964) *I Never Promised You a Rose Garden*, New York, New American Library. *80*

Greenberg, I.A. (1974) *Psychodrama: Theory and Therapy*, London, Souvenir Press. *93*

Guntrip, H. (1969) *Schizoid Phenomena, Object-Relations and the Self*, New York, International Universities Press. *22*

Haley, J. (1963) *Strategies of Psychotherapy*, New York, Grune & Stratton. *27, 41, 52, 64*

Heaton, J. (1979) 'Theory in psychotherapy', in Bolton N. (ed.) *Philosophical Problems in Psychology*, London, Methuen. *65, 68*

Heaton, J. (1982) 'Freud and Heidegger on the interpretation of slips of the tongue', *Journal of the British Society for Phenomenology*, 13, 129–42.

Heidegger, M. (1954) *What is Called Thinking*, trans. F.D. Wieck and J.G. Gray, New York, Harper & Row. *152*

Heraclitus, in Kirk, G.S. and Raven, J.E. (eds) (1957) *The Presocratic Philosophers*, Cambridge, Cambridge University Press. *145*

Herink, R. (1980) *The Psychotherapy Handbook*, New York, Meridian. *44*

Homer, *Iliad*, with trans. by A.T. Murray (1924) Loeb Classical Library, London, Heinemann. *31–7, 43, 51, 68*

Horney, K. (1942) *Self-analysis*, London, Routledge & Kegan Paul. *69*

Ingleby, D. (1981) 'Understanding mental illness', in Ingleby, D. (ed.) *Critical Psychiatry: the Politics of Mental Health*, Harmondsworth, Penguin. *25, 64*

Jaynes, J. (1976) *The Origin of Consciousness in the Breakdown of the Bicameral Mind*, London, Allen Lane. *31–4, 41, 43*

Katz, J.M. (1980) 'Discrepancy, arousal and labelling: towards a psychosocial theory of emotion', *Sociological Inquiry*, 50, 147–56. *137*

Kelman, H.C. (1963) 'The role of the group in the induction of therapeutic change', *International Journal of Group Psychotherapy*, 13, 399–432. *128–9*

Khan, M.M.R. (1972) 'The finding and becoming of self', in Khan, M.M.R. *The Privacy of the Self*, London, Hogarth, 294–305. *151*

Kierkegaard, S. (1844) *The Concept of Dread*, trans. W. Lowrie, Princeton, NJ, Princeton University Press. *125*

Kierkegaard, S. (1846) *Concluding Unscientific Postscript*, trans. D.F. Swenson and W. Lowrie, Princeton, NJ, Princeton University Press. *69–70*

Kierkegaard, S. (1849) *The Sickness unto Death*, trans. W. Lowrie, Princeton, NJ, Princeton University Press. *136*

Klein, M. (1955) 'The psychoanalytic play technique: its history and significance', in Klein, M., Heiman, P. and Monty-Kyrle, R. (eds) *New Directions in Psychoanalysis*, London, Tavistock. *141*

Koestler, A. (1979) *Janus: a Summing Up*, New York, Vantage. *11*

Kovel, J. (1976) *A Complete Guide to Therapy*, Harmondsworth, Pelican. *44*

Lacan, J. (1966) *Ecrits: a Selection*, trans. A. Sheridan, London, Tavistock. *43, 57, 145–51, 154*

Laing, R.D. (1967) *The Politics of Experience*, Harmondsworth, Penguin. *43, 57, 144*

Laing, R.D., Phillipson, H. and Lee, A.R. (1966) *Interpersonal Perception: a Theory and a Method of Research*, London, Tavistock. *138*

Lang, P.J. (1970) 'Stimulus control, response control, and the desensitization of fear', in Levis, D.J. (ed.) *Learning Approaches to Therapeutic Behavior Change*, Chicago, Aldine. *79*

Laplanche, J. and Pontalis, J.-B (1973) *The Language of Psychoanalysis*, trans. D. Nicholson-Smith, London, Hogarth. *62–3*

Lévi-Strauss, C. (1955) *Tristes Tropiques*, trans. J. and D. Weightman, Harmondsworth, Penguin. *122*

Lewis, H.R. and Streitfield, H.S. (1970) *Growth Games*, London, Abacus. *95*

Lieberman, M.A., Yalom, I.D. and Miles, M.B. (1973) *Encounter Groups: First Facts*, New York, Basic Books. *7–16, 118, 120, 123, 126*

Luborsky, L., Singer, B. and Luborsky, L. (1975) 'Comparative studies of psychotherapies', *Archives of General Psychiatry* 32, 995–1008. *81*

Luft, J. (1963) *Group Processes*, Palo Alto, California, National Press. *123*

Malan, D. (1979) *Individual Psychotherapy and the Science of Psychodynamics*, London, Butterworths. *62*

Mathews, A.M., Gelder, M.G. and Johnston, D.W. (1981) *Agoraphobia: Nature and Treatment*, London, Tavistock. *46*

Mead, G.H. (1912) 'The mechanism of social consciousness', in Rack, A.J. (ed.) (1964) *Selected Writings: G.H. Mead*, Indianapolis, Bobbs-Merrill, 134–41. *19–25, 146*

Mead, G.H. (1913) 'The social self', in Rack, A.J. (ed.) (1964) *Selected Writings: G.H. Mead*, Indianapolis, Bobbs-Merrill, 142–9. *22, 50*

Mead, G.H. (1924–5) 'The genesis of the self and social control', in Rack, A.J. (ed.) (1964) *Selected Writings: G.H. Mead*, Indianapolis, Bobbs-Merrill, 267–93. *21, 146*

Merleau-Ponty, M. (1960) 'The child's relations with others', in Merleau-Ponty, M., *The Primacy of Perception*, Evanston, Ill., Northwestern University Press. *151*

Minuchin, S. and Fishman, H.C. (1981) *Family Therapy Techniques*, Cambridge, Mass., Harvard University Press. *11, 19*

Mitchell, J. (1982) 'Introduction', in Mitchell, J. and Rose, J. (eds) *Feminine Sexuality: Jaques Lacan and the Ecole Freudienne*, London, Macmillan. *147*

Mitchell, J. and Rose, J. (1982) *Feminine Sexuality: Jaques Lacan and the Ecole Freudienne*, London, Macmillan. *147*

Miura, I. and Sasaki, R.F. (1965) *The Zen Koan: Its History and Use in Rinzai Zen*, New York, Harcourt, Brace and World. *158-9*

Moreno, J.L. (1940) 'Mental catharsis and the psychodrama', *Sociometry*, 1, 209-44. *93-5, 129, 141*

Oatley, K. (1980) 'Theories of personal learning in groups', in Smith, P.B. (ed.) *Small Groups and Personal Change*, London, Methuen. *124*

Oatley, K. (1981a) 'Representing ourselves: mental schemata, computational metaphors and the nature of consciousness', in Underwood, G. and Stevens, R. (eds) *Aspects of Consciousness*, vol. 2, London, Academic Press, 87-117. *72*

Oatley, K. (1981b) 'The self with others: the person and the interpersonal context in the approaches of C.R. Rogers and R.D. Laing', in Fransella, F. (ed.) *Personality: Theory, Measurement and Research*, London, Methuen, 191-207. *58*

Oatley, K. (1982) 'Refutation and the appropriation of truth in psychoanalysis', *British Journal of Medical Psychology*, 55, 1-11. *86, 131*

Pfister, G. (1975) 'Outcomes of laboratory training for police officers', *Journal of Social Issues*, 31, 115-21. *117*

Plato, *The Symposium*, trans. W. Hamilton, Harmondsworth, Penguin. *6*

Plato, *Phaedrus and Letters VII and VIII*, trans. W. Hamilton, Harmondsworth, Penguin. *5-8, 68*

Rachman, S.J. (1971) *The Effects of Psychotherapy*, Oxford, Pergamon. *81*

Rachman, S.J. and Wilson, G.T. (1980) *The Effects of Psychological Therapy*, 2nd edn, Oxford, Pergamon. *79*

Reed, D. (1976) *Anna*, Harmondsworth, Penguin. *80*

Rogers, C.R. (1951) *Client-centred Therapy*, London, Constable. *57, 74*

Rogers, C.R. (1961) *On Becoming a Person: a Therapist's View of Psychotherapy*, London, Constable. *58-9, 74-5, 87, 89, 116*

Rogers, C.R. (1968) 'Interpersonal relationships: USA 2000', *Journal of Applied Behavioral Science*, 4, 265-80. *88*

Rogers, C.R. (1970) *Encounter Groups*, Harmondsworth, Pelican. *157*

Ryle, A. (1982) *Psychotherapy: a Cognitive Integration of Theory and Practice*, London, Academic Press. *41, 50, 68, 112*

Schreiber, F.R. (1973) *Sybil*, Harmondsworth, Penguin. *80*

Schutz, W.C. (1971) *Here Comes Everybody*, New York, Harper & Row. *94*

Shaffer, J.P.B. and Galinsky, M.D. (1974) *Models of Group Therapy and Sensitivity Training*, Englewood Cliffs, NJ, Prentice-Hall. *93*

Shapiro, D.A. (1980) 'Science and psychotherapy: the state of the art', *British Journal of Medical Psychology*, 53, 1–10. *83, 86*

Simon, B. (1978) *Mind and Madness in Ancient Greece: the Classical Roots of Modern Psychiatry*, Ithaca, Cornell University Press. *34*

Slater, E. and Roth, M. (1977) *Clinical Psychiatry*, 3rd edn, revised, London, Ballière Tindall and Cassell. *25*

Sloane, R.B., Staples, F.R., Cristol, A.H., Yorkston, N.J. and Whipple, K. (1975) *Psychotherapy versus Behavior Therapy*, Cambridge, Mass., Harvard University Press. *76–7, 84–5, 109*

Smith, M.L., Glass, G.V. and Miller, T.I. (1980) *The Benefits of Psychotherapy*, Baltimore, Johns Hopkins Press. *80–7, 106, 118*

Smith, P.B. (1975) 'Are there adverse effects of sensitivity training?', *Journal of Humanistic Psychology*, 15, 29–48. *110*

Smith, P.B. (1980a) *Group Processes and Personal Change*, London, Harper & Row. *117–18, 128*

Smith, P.B. (ed.) (1980b) *Small Groups and Personal Change*, London, Methuen. *117–18*

Smith, P.B. (1980c) 'An attributional analysis of personal learning', in Alderfer, C.P. and Cooper, C.L. (eds) *Advances in Experiential Processes*, vol. 2, Chichester, Wiley, 63–92. *128–9*

Smith, P.B. (1981) 'Research into humanistic personality theories', in Fransella, F. (ed.) *Personality: Theory, Measurement and Research*, London, Methuen, 208–21. *74–5*

Smith, P.B., Wood, H. and Smale, G.G. (1980) 'The usefulness of groups in clinical settings', in Smith, P.B. (ed.) *Small Groups and Personal Change*, London, Methuen, 106–53. *106*

Snell, B. (1953) *The Discovery of the Mind*, New York, Harper & Row. *31*

Strachey, J. (1934) 'The nature of the therapeutic action of psychoanalysis', *International Journal of Psychoanalysis*, 15, 127–59. *95*

Sullivan, H.S. (1953) *The Interpersonal Theory of Psychiatry*, New York, Norton. *83*

Szasz, T.S. (1965) *The Ethics of Psychoanalysis: the Theory and Method of Autonomous Psychotherapy*, New York, Basic Books. *70, 125*

Totman, R. (1976a) 'Cognitive dissonance and the placebo response', *European Journal of Social Psychology*, 5, 119–25. *74–5*

Totman, R. (1976b) 'Cognitive dissonance and the placebo treatment of insomnia – a pilot experiment', *British Journal of Medical Psychology*, 49, 393–400. *55*

Totman, R. (1979) *Social Causes of Illness*, London, Souvenir Press. *55*

Totman, R. (1982) 'Philosophical foundations of attribution therapies', in

Antalsi, C. and Brewin, C. (eds) *Attribution and Psychological Change*, London, Academic Press. *54–8, 64, 126*

Totman, R. (1984) *A Theory of Society, Action and Health*, London, Academic Press. *54*

Truax, C.B. and Mitchell, K.M. (1971) 'Research on certain therapist interpersonal skills in relation to process and outcome', in Bergin, A.E. and Garfield, S.L. (eds) *Handbook of Psychotherapy and Behavior Change: an Empirical Analysis*, New York, Wiley. *74–111*

Watts, A. (1966) *The Book: On the Taboo Against Knowing Who You Are*, New York, Vintage. *12*

Whyte, L.L. (1978) *The Unconscious Before Freud*, London, Friedmann. *66*

Winnicott, D.W. (1971) *Playing and Reality*, Harmondsworth, Penguin. *vii, 94, 124, 140–2, 144–5, 149, 154*

Winnicott, D.W. (1979) *The Maturational Processes and the Facilitating Environment: Studies in the Theory of Emotional Development*, London, Hogarth. *22, 140–2, 144–5*

Wolpe, J. (1958) *Psychotherapy by Reciprocal Inhibition*, Stanford, Stanford University Press. *66*

Subject index

agency, 3, 36, 55–6, 117, 148
agoraphobia, 18–19, 28, 35, 45
alienation, 25, 112, 144, 147–9
anxiety, 8–9, 18–19, 25, 33, 35, 41, 45–8, 51, 58, 78–9, 83, 90, 112, 136–7, 140
authenticity, 2, 3, 71, 126
autonomy: see individuality

Buddhism, 8, 152–3

cases: *aliquis*, 38–9, 42; Mr Hal D, 59–65, 69, 95, 139; Ms Emma H, 89–91, 99–105, 113, 116, 124, 129, 132–3, 139; Ms Cindy S, 8–9, 18–19, 28–9, 35, 40–2, 44–56, 64, 68–9, 139; woman of the theatre dream, 39–40, 42; the writer, 136–7, 139
causal explanation, 66, 67, 85, 87, 129
cognitive dissonance, 54–6, 126, 130
communication: direct and indirect, 5–7, 69–70, 151
community, 2–4, 10–29, 66–7, 154
compliance, 128–9, 142–3, 145

condensation, 41–2, 63
consciousness, 17, 21, 31–4, 36, 43, 48, 68, 123
control, 9, 13, 17, 18, 23–5, 37, 52, 134, 144, 146–8
control groups in outcome studies, 81–2, 109, 115–18
coping, 111–13, 115–16, 151
creativity, 136, 140–5, 154
culture, 121–3, 135–55

defensiveness, 58, 69, 91, 112–13, 117, 123, 131, 138–9, 145
depression (despair), 9, 19, 24–5, 27, 35, 41, 50–1, 60–1, 78, 133
desire (wishes), 36, 39, 41–2, 58, 63, 67, 133, 141, 146, 149
diagnosis, 34–5, 127
difference, 7, 112–13, 29, 151
disappointment, vii, 22–3, 25, 56, 60–3, 103–4, 113, 124, 129, 133, 142, 149–50
displacement, 41–2

165

disturbance: by the Other, 146–7; of conversation, 39; psychosomatic, 32–3; to others, 2, 18, 35, 43; to self, 2, 18, 35; symptomatic, 36–7

drama (theatre), 1, 15, 21, 22, 61, 93–6, 105, 127, 140–1

dreams, 37, 39–40, 60–1, 64, 77, 147

ego, 12, 66, 145–9

emotions (feelings), 25, 30–5, 36–7, 41, 42, 50, 59, 79, 88, 92, 129, 131, 135–55

engagement (engrossment), 2, 15–18, 27, 66

ethos, 65–6, 121, 131

experience, 10–15, 17, 19–20, 23, 24–5, 31–2, 37, 44, 55, 59, 64, 88–94, 108, 122, 124–5, 135, 144, 150–2

free association, 37–9, 41, 94, 141

games, 4, 13–17, 21, 27, 37, 63, 90, 95–7, 100–1, 144

groups: benefits of, 108, 113–19; casualties in, 108–11, 126; comparison with individual therapy, 84, 152; culture of, 97–9, 121–2; definition of, 92; encounter, 93, 107, 108, 117; evaluation of effects of, 106–19; experience in, 89–94, 99–105; experiential learning in, 124–7; games in, 95–7; leadership of, 90–1, 95, 107–8, 111–14, 120–1, 126–7; origins of, 92–4; psychodrama, 93–5, 103–5, 107; safety and challenge in, 127–35, 143; sensitivity, 88, 107, 117; T-groups, 88, 107, 117; types of change from, 115, 117–18; varieties of, 88

hiddenness, 123–4, 144

holons, 11, 13, 17

'I' and 'me', 19–24, 124, 145, 148, 151, 152, 154

identification, 128–9

imaginary, the, 148

individuality, 2–5, 17–18, 30–43, 56–7, 154

internalization, 128–9

interpretation, 36–40, 60, 64, 70, 79, 95, 114, 122, 140, 143, 151

involuntary, the, 16, 24–5, 36–43, 69, 146, 147

koans, 152–3

language: and groups, 92; of derogation, 127; of *Iliad*, 32–5, 43; of mental events, 36–43; of symptoms, 24, 52, 64, 151; the order of, 142, 145

lapses (slips, parapraxes), 17–18, 36–9, 43, 70, 147

learning, 70, 108, 111, 114–16, 118, 134

love, 144, 148–50

mind, 10, 11, 18, 32–4, 39, 41, 43

name of the father, 145–7

openness, 115, 123

owning and disowning actions, 8, 15, 28, 31, 42, 54–6, 129, 133

participation, 13–18, 21, 27, 92, 106, 117, 138, 145, 148, 150, 152, 154–5

patriarchy, 145–6, 149–50, 155

perceptions of others, 117, 123–4, 132, 146–7, 149–50

personality, 35

placebo, 55, 93–5

play, 5, 13–21, 27, 37, 70, 90, 94, 96–9, 129, 133–5, 140–5, 148, 150, 153–4

power, 3, 13, 25, 28, 42, 53, 149, 155

preoccupation, 16, 18, 20, 27, 39, 101, 124

projection, 131–3, 137, 140, 149–50

psychiatry, 17, 25, 34–5, 136

psychoanalysis, 19, 22–4, 36–43, 57–64, 73, 76–80, 82–3, 86, 95, 107, 145, 148

recognition, 72, 143–5

reification, 12, 19–20, 24, 64–5, 69, 71, 145, 149

relationships: complementary, 26, 29, 52, 63, 127, 130; containment and support in, 70, 113, 127–31; internalization of, 20–5, 128, 140–2; loss of, 25, 137; marital, 29, 54, 101, 136, 138–40; prevention of, 127; sexual, 41, 60, 99, 101, 148–50; symmetrical, 63, 130; with parents, 21–3, 58, 60, 64, 128, 140–2, 145–7, 149–50

relaxation training, 47, 54, 77

repression, 128

resistance, 62–4

responsibility, 28, 42, 52, 56, 87, 116, 120, 133

right action, 2, 6, 65, 70–2, 125

roles, 14, 19, 21, 22, 24, 28, 29, 63, 93, 96,

121, 129, 132, 145, 146

rules: and creativity, 154; and meaning, 4, 14–15, 66–7; discussion of, in groups, 92; mutuality of, 130, 137–40; negotiation of, 27–9, 52–4, 64, 98, 138, 143; of a community, 2, 4, 13, 21; of families, 4, 11, 19, 140; of a game, 14, 21; of relationships, 27–9, 130, 140; personal, 138–9; regulative and constitutive, 68–70, 85, 122–3

scripts, 23–4, 63, 94–5, 130, 145
self, 4, 10, 11–13, 19–24, 29, 32–7, 41, 43, 58, 130–1, 137; 'know thyself', 7, 43, 92, 126; revelation of, 123–4; true and false, 122, 144–5, 147
self-concept, 117
self-esteem, 83, 87, 110, 115, 117, 118
self-experience, 150–2
sex roles, 149–50
sexuality, 148–50
social influence, 54–6, 126, 128–9
society (see also rules): and culture, 121–3, 141–2; inequalities of, 25; membership of, 3, 13, 21, 122; place in, 24–5
space in between self and other, 5, 87, 134, 136, 140, 142, 151
splitting, 23, 26, 145, 147, 149–50
strategies and tactics, 22–3, 27–9, 39, 52, 63–4, 68–9, 116
symbolic order, 145–6
symptoms, 9, 11, 16–19, 23–9, 151; as involuntary disturbances, 36–43, 51; as language to be understood, 24, 52, 64; as tactics, 27–9, 52; assessment of, 77–9, 106; hierarchy of, 34–6; prevalence of, 24–5; psychosomatic, 33, 51
systematic desensitization, 46–7, 82

theory: attribution, 54–6, 126, 128–30; object-relations, 19, 22–4, 64, 132, 146, 148, 150; of consciousness, 31–4; of identity, 31–4; of meaning, 15; of the involuntary, 37–43; of therapeutic

practice, 51–4, 64–72, 126–34, 140–5; personal compared with scientific, 131–2
therapists' effectiveness, 75, 84, 111–14, 118–19, 126–7
therapy (psychotherapy): as changing personal theories, 131–4; as dialogue with symptoms, 25; as discovering meaning, 26, 72, 113, 129, 143 (see also interpretation); as ethical activity, 2, 64–72, 130, 153; as experiential learning, 125–7; as meta-education, 70. 74, 125; as play, vii, 94, 133–4, 140–4, 152; as political, 26; as reflection on personal rules, 68–70; as relationship, 1, 5, 7, 51–4, 85; as reowning, 42, 133; as support plus challenge, 127–31, 143; behavioural, 46, 51, 57, 75–9, 81–3, 128; client-centred, 58–9, 87; cognitive-behavioural, 45–54, 57, 83; decision to undertake, 29, 73; definitions, 5, 8, 37, 65, 82; directive, 44–57, 66, 68, 72, 75, 152; effects compared with drugs, 84–5; examples in progress, 47–50, 59–62, 99–105; existential-phenomenological, 57, 59, 64–73, 80; harm from, 108–113; humanistic, 94–5, 108, 118; individual v. group, 2, 84, 106, 108; lastingness of, 78, 108, 116–18; measurement of outcome of, 73–87, 106–19; meta-analysis of, 81–5, 106; non-directive, 44, 57–64, 66, 68, 71–3, 75, 152; non-specific effects of, 83–5; psychoanalytic, 59–64, 75, 77–80, 82–3; purpose of, 26, 140–1, 153–5; reasons for seeking, 9, 16, 19, 153
thoughts, 32–4, 49–50, 57, 92
transference, 62–4, 140–1
transitional phenomena, 141–2

unconscious, the, 17–19, 32, 36–43, 123, 147, 148

wholeness, 1, 2, 4, 5, 11, 23, 37, 43, 145, 146

At present in European and American history, men are dismayed that *man*kind is no longer to be seen as all there is, but that men are just part of our race of beings. Men's arrogance is subverted by the part that women play. Women are no longer prepared to play a part that seems to have been assigned to them by men, but which functions to mirror men back to themselves. Women sense the possibility of another part, their own.

In a coexisting thread of Soviet–American history, two superpowers, each apparently enraged by being only part, not all, confront each other and suggest the answer might be to destroy the whole lot.

To be part, to take part, to participate in culture is, for us mortals, all there is.

ferences and name index

italics following each entry refer to page numbers in this book.

1964) *Dibs: In Search of Self*, Harmondsworth, Pelican. *80*
6) *The Duality of Human Existence: Isolation and Communion*
lan, Boston, Beacon. *3*
935) 'Culture, contact and schismogenesis', reprinted in
3) 35–46. *63, 130*
955) 'A theory of play and fantasy', reprinted in Bateson
. *104*
70) 'Form, substance and difference', reprinted in Bate-
–40. *12–13*
971) 'The cybernetics of self: a theory of alcoholism',
Bateson (1973) 280–308. *10–13, 21, 28, 66*
73) *Steps to an Ecology of Mind*, St Albans, Paladin. *125*
Gordon, B. (1972) 'The value of encounter', in Solomon,
on, B. (eds) *New Perspectives on Encounter Groups*, San
ssey-Bass. *110*
6) *Cognitive Therapy and the Emotional Disorders*, New
an. *50*

Suggestions for further reading

Chapter 1

Bakan, D. (1966) *The Duality of Human Existence: Isolation and Communion in Western Man*, Boston, Beacon.
Kovel, J. (1976) *A Complete Guide to Therapy*, Harmondsworth, Pelican.
Plato, *The Symposium*, trans. W. Hamilton, Harmondsworth, Penguin.

Chapter 2

Bateson, G. (1973) *Steps to an Ecology of Mind*, St Albans, Paladin.
Goffman, E. (1961) *Encounters: Two Studies in the Sociology of Interaction*, Indianapolis, Bobbs-Merrill.
Haley, J. (1963) *Strategies of Psychotherapy*, New York, Grune & Stratton.

Chapter 3

Freud, S. (1901) *The Psychopathology of Everyday Life*, trans. A. Tyson, Pelican Freud Library, vol. 5, Harmondsworth, Pelican.
Jaynes, J. (1976) *The Origin of Consciousness in the Breakdown of the Bicameral Mind*, London, Allen Lane.

Chapter 4

Freud, S. (1905) *Case Histories, 1: D*
J. Strachey, Pelican Freud Library
Rogers, C.R. (1961) *On Becoming a*
therapy, London, Constable.
Ryle, A. (1982) *Psychotherapy: a Cogn*
London, Academic Press.

Chapter 5

Schreiber, F.R. (1973) *Sybil*, Harm
Sloane, R.B., Staples, F.R., Cris
ple, K. (1975) *Psychotherapy ve*
Mass., Harvard University Pres
Smith, M.L., Glass, G.V. and Mi
therapy, Baltimore, Johns Hopk

Chapter 6

Rogers, C.R. (1970) *Encounter Gr*
Shaffer, J.P.B. and Galinsky, M
Sensitivity Training, Englewoo

Chapter 7

Lieberman, M.A., Yalom, I.D.
First Facts, New York, Basic
Smith, P.B. (1980a) *Group Proce*
& Row.

Chapter 8

Smith, P.B. (ed.) (1980b) *Sm*
Methuen.

Chapter 9

Dinnerstein, D. (1976) *The R*
London, Souvenir Press.
Gallop, J. (1982) *Feminism*
London, Macmillan.
Winnicott, D.W. (1971) *Play*

The numbers

Axline, V.M.
Bakan, D. (19
  in Western
Bateson, G.
  Bateson (19
Bateson, G.
  (1973) 150–
Bateson, G. (
  son (1973) 4
Bateson, G.
  reprinted in
Bateson, G. (
Bebout, J. and
  L. and Ber
  Francisco, J.
Beck, A.T. (
  York, Merid

At present in European and American history, men are dismayed that *man*kind is no longer to be seen as all there is, but that men are just part of our race of beings. Men's arrogance is subverted by the part that women play. Women are no longer prepared to play a part that seems to have been assigned to them by men, but which functions to mirror men back to themselves. Women sense the possibility of another part, their own.

In a coexisting thread of Soviet–American history, two superpowers, each apparently enraged by being only part, not all, confront each other and suggest the answer might be to destroy the whole lot.

To be part, to take part, to participate in culture is, for us mortals, all there is.

Suggestions for further reading

Chapter 1

Bakan, D. (1966) *The Duality of Human Existence: Isolation and Communion in Western Man*, Boston, Beacon.
Kovel, J. (1976) *A Complete Guide to Therapy*, Harmondsworth, Pelican.
Plato, *The Symposium*, trans. W. Hamilton, Harmondsworth, Penguin.

Chapter 2

Bateson, G. (1973) *Steps to an Ecology of Mind*, St Albans, Paladin.
Goffman, E. (1961) *Encounters: Two Studies in the Sociology of Interaction*, Indianapolis, Bobbs-Merrill.
Haley, J. (1963) *Strategies of Psychotherapy*, New York, Grune & Stratton.

Chapter 3

Freud, S. (1901) *The Psychopathology of Everyday Life*, trans. A. Tyson, Pelican Freud Library, vol. 5, Harmondsworth, Pelican.
Jaynes, J. (1976) *The Origin of Consciousness in the Breakdown of the Bicameral Mind*, London, Allen Lane.

Chapter 4

Freud, S. (1905) *Case Histories, 1: Dora and Little Hans*, trans. A. and J. Strachey, Pelican Freud Library, vol. 8, Harmondsworth, Pelican.

Rogers, C.R. (1961) *On Becoming a Person: a Therapist's View of Psychotherapy*, London, Constable.

Ryle, A. (1982) *Psychotherapy: a Cognitive Integration of Theory and Practice*, London, Academic Press.

Chapter 5

Schreiber, F.R. (1973) *Sybil*, Harmondsworth, Penguin.

Sloane, R.B., Staples, F.R., Cristol, A.H., Yorkston, N.J. and Whipple, K. (1975) *Psychotherapy versus Behaviour Therapy*, Cambridge, Mass., Harvard University Press.

Smith, M.L., Glass, G.V. and Miller, T.I. (1980) *The Benefits of Psychotherapy*, Baltimore, Johns Hopkins Press.

Chapter 6

Rogers, C.R. (1970) *Encounter Groups*, Harmondsworth, Pelican.

Shaffer, J.P.B. and Galinsky, M.D. (1974) *Models of Group Therapy and Sensitivity Training*, Englewood Cliffs, NJ, Prentice-Hall.

Chapter 7

Lieberman, M.A., Yalom, I.D. and Miles, M.B. (1973) *Encounter Groups: First Facts*, New York, Basic Books.

Smith, P.B. (1980a) *Group Processes and Personal Change*, London, Harper & Row.

Chapter 8

Smith, P.B. (ed.) (1980b) *Small Groups and Personal Change*, London, Methuen.

Chapter 9

Dinnerstein, D. (1976) *The Rocking of the Cradle and the Ruling of the World*, London, Souvenir Press.

Gallop, J. (1982) *Feminism and Psychoanalysis: the Daughter's Seduction*, London, Macmillan.

Winnicott, D.W. (1971) *Playing and Reality*, Harmondsworth, Penguin.

References and name index

The numbers in italics following each entry refer to page numbers in this book.

Axline, V.M. (1964) *Dibs: In Search of Self*, Harmondsworth, Pelican. *80*

Bakan, D. (1966) *The Duality of Human Existence: Isolation and Communion in Western Man*, Boston, Beacon. *3*

Bateson, G. (1935) 'Culture, contact and schismogenesis', reprinted in Bateson (1973) 35–46. *63, 130*

Bateson, G. (1955) 'A theory of play and fantasy', reprinted in Bateson (1973) 150–66. *104*

Bateson, G. (1970) 'Form, substance and difference', reprinted in Bateson (1973) 423–40. *12–13*

Bateson, G. (1971) 'The cybernetics of self: a theory of alcoholism', reprinted in Bateson (1973) 280–308. *10–13, 21, 28, 66*

Bateson, G. (1973) *Steps to an Ecology of Mind*, St Albans, Paladin. *125*

Bebout, J. and Gordon, B. (1972) 'The value of encounter', in Solomon, L. and Berzon, B. (eds) *New Perspectives on Encounter Groups*, San Francisco, Jossey-Bass. *110*

Beck, A.T. (1976) *Cognitive Therapy and the Emotional Disorders*, New York, Meridian. *50*